Southern Living

ideas for great
WINDOW
TREATMENTS

For a dressier-than-usual family room, curtains are silk, but left unlined and shirred on rods to relax their formality.

Oxmoor House®

Gathered valances sport a natty trim of jumbo welt (for another view, see pages 38–39).

Southern Living® Ideas for Great Window Treatments was adapted from a book by the same title published by Sunset Books.

Book Editor
Lynne Gilberg

Research & Text
Christine Barnes, Susan Lang

Coordinating Editor
Linda J. Selden

Consulting Editor
Jane Horn

Editorial Coordinators
Bradford Kachelhofer, Vicki Weathers

Design
Joe di Chiarro

Illustrations
Susan Jaekel

Photo Styling
Sudi Scull, JoAnn Masaoka Van Atta

Special Contributors
Linda Bouchard, Bridget Biscotti Bradley, Barbara Brown, Tishana Peebles, Jean Warboy

Cover
Design: **James Boone, Vasken Guiragossian**. Photography: **Sylvia Martin, Southern Progress Photo Collection**. Interior Designer: **Fern Smith**

Our appreciation to the staff of *Southern Living* magazine for their contributions to this book.

Southern Living® is a federally registered trademark of Southern Living, Inc.

10 9 8 7 6 5 4 3 2
First printing January 2000
Copyright © 2000 by Oxmoor House, Inc.
Book Division of Southern Progress Corporation
P.O. Box 2463
Birmingham, Alabama 35201
All rights reserved, including the right of reproduction in whole or in part in any form.

ISBN 0-376-09078-2
Library of Congress Catalog Card Number: 99-65029
Printed in the United States

Photographers: Jean Allsopp, 6–7, 8, 18 bottom; **Ardon Armstrong,** 67 top; **Tim Beavis,** 53 top **Danmer, Inc.,** 48; **ETM Studios,** 14 bottom, 49 bottom, 88 right, 91; **Philip Harvey**, 2, 5 right, 9, 10 bottom, 13 top, 14 top, 16 bottom, 17 top, 18 top, 28, 29, 34 top, 38, 40, 41, 42, 43, 44, 45, 46 left, 47, 51 right top, 52, 53 bottom, 55 left and top right, 56 tp left and right, 57 58, 59 bottom, 60, 63, 64 bottom, 68 bottom, 69 left and top right, 89, back cover top; **Louis Joyner,** 12 bottom, 64 top; **LouverDrape,** 15 top, 50, 51 left; **Sylvia Martin,** 12 top, 16 top right, 54, 61 (both); **Jack McDowell,** 75 top left; **Colin McRae,** 70, 72, 75 bottom, 76, 77, 78, 81, 82, 83, 84, 86, 87, 88 left, 92; **Art Meripol,** 67 bottom; **Emily Minton,** 1, 66 bottom, back cover bottom; **John O'Hagan,** 5 left, 17 bottom, 46 right, 56 bottom, 59 top, 65, 66 top; back cover bottom; **Norman A. Plate,** 68 top; **Cheryl Sales,** 13 bottom, 15 bottom, 49 top, 55 bottom right, 62 top, 69 bottom right; **Meg McKinney Simle,** 33 right, 34 bottom, 51 bottom right; **Waverly,** 10 top; **Russ Widstrand,** 75 top right; **Tom Wyatt,** 27.

Wonderful Windows

Something exciting happens when you dress your windows in new window treatments. Whatever the style of your home, new window coverings have the power to enliven or even transform a room. But how do you bring about that transformation?

This book provides the inspiration and information you'll need to help you choose the right window treatments—and to have fun doing it. Start with the descriptions of the options available to you. Then browse through the photo section to see a myriad of successful treatments. Finally, turn to the shopping guide for help in making your selections, whether you're looking for the newest energy-efficient glass or the latest in decorative hardware.

We thank the following people for sharing their expertise with us and for providing props for use in the photographs: The Auxiliary of the Volunteer Center of Marin, Marin Designer Showcase; Diane Burrell of Southern Accents magazine; Rick Burris of Burris Window Shades; The Coyote Point Museum Auxiliary Carolands Decorators' Show House; Larry De La Cruz and John Mott of Decorator's Walk; Paul Eisenberg of Poppy Fabrics; Maryann Ewing; Joyce Grimley of National Glass Association; Harding's Nevada City Interiors; Muffy Hook; Greg Irving of Pella/Rolscreen; Brad Lange of Pacific Showrooms West, Inc.

Also, Marina Continental Window Coverings; Judy Marrocco of Glass Block Designs; Hamilton Montgomery of Montgomery Designs; Katherine Pearson of Southern Living magazine; Joe Remmert of Ohline Corp.; Steve Selkowitz and Dariush Arasteh of Lawrence Berkeley Laboratory; Dan Smith of Charles Minne, Inc.; John Stickney of Hunter Douglas Window Fashions; Jeanne Tepper; Jill Van de Wege; and Jerry Victor of V & W Patio Door & Window Company, Inc.

Special thanks go to Fran Feldman for carefully editing the manuscript.

CONTENTS

WINDOW DRESSING   5

A PLANNING PRIMER   7

GREAT WINDOW TREATMENTS   39

A SHOPPER'S GUIDE   71

INDEX   96

SPECIAL FEATURES

Sheet Smart   9

Decorative Details   11

On-the-Spot Tops   19

Window Seats   27

Energy Savers   30

Visual Effects   35

A Window Treatment Questionnaire   37

Linings: The Inside Story   80

Installing Curtain & Drapery Rods   85

Putting Up Shades, Blinds & Shutters   90

Care & Cleaning Tips   93

Information Sources   94

WINDOW DRESSING

Although much has changed in window treatments recently, many of today's popular styles are really nothing new. From earliest times, people have been covering their windows to keep out the cold, first with skins and later with such coverings as crude wood shutters and simple tapestries. By the 16th century, single curtain panels attached to rings were basic window wear.

As cultures acquired wealth, windows and their treatments took on more importance. In the 17th century, rich upholstered cornices appeared, along with pull-up shades, the forerunners of today's fabric shades. The next two centuries produced a wealth of styles—draperies, Venetian blinds, swags and cascades, and decorative poles and finials—that still find favor today.

Technological advances in fibers and design are taking window coverings into the 21st century. Energy-efficient shades, glazing, and window frames crowd the market, with new products being introduced constantly. Elegant curtains that puddle on the floor, tapered valances that tame the deep folds of formal draperies, and stately swags and cascades provide design drama, wrapping windows in flowing fabric and beautifully framing the view beyond. Still popular are shutters, with their classic narrow louvers or with wide slats that command attention.

No matter which covering you choose, a well-designed window treatment is built on a solid foundation, one that involves planning, inspiration, and knowledge. For planning help, turn to the first chapter for a rundown of all the window treatment options, ways to determine your individual needs, and some basic decorating principles.

As you begin to narrow down your choices, use the photos that follow to visualize how different treatments will look on your windows. Notice that some of the most successful treatments are achieved by combining several different options for a coordinated look.

Finally, turn to the shopping guide (pages 71–95) for specific product information and shopping tips. In no time at all, your fresh, new window treatments will be dressing up the windows of your home.

DESIGN: MARY CASON

Elaborate tassel fringe and oversized tassels on tiebacks define the shape and echo the muted hues of multicolored silk curtains.

Graceful plantation shutters invite the outdoors in, joining interior and exterior spaces.

perfect match to the timeless rchitecture and contemporary uches of this sophisticated living om, the window panels are rich brics treated in an elegant, yet sual style.

5

INTERIOR DESIGNER: SHARON M. GILKEY

A PLANNING PRIMER

Looking to freshen up a room's decor? Eager to emphasize a beautiful view? Trying to disguise some not-so-attractive windows? Window treatments can do all this and more—that is, if you know how to choose the one that's right for your situation.

Begin right here, with basic information on the myriad styles of window treatments available on the market today. Note which coverings work best on different windows. Then use the practical tips and decorating guidelines at the end of the chapter to plan the treatment that works for you.

The owners felt no need to fully cover the windows of this master bedroom sitting area. Fabric panels with elegant rope and tassel trim hang below the arch of the windows, allowing in light, but ensuring privacy.

7

DECORATING YOUR WINDOWS

One glance at a home decorating magazine will convince you that there's been a virtual explosion in window treatments lately. Such innovative products as cellular shades, extra-wide rods, and vertical blinds compete with the traditional and familiar curtains and draperies. And imaginative top treatments now transform even the tried-and-true styles into sensational window coverings.

With all the choices both old and new, it's easy to feel overwhelmed. For guidance, start by acquainting yourself with the wonderful array of window coverings now on the market.

CURTAINS

Once considered strictly casual, curtains have now earned a place in even the most elegant interiors. That's not to say that informal curtains are relics of the past; rather, the choices are now wonderfully varied, from short cafés to billowy floor-length panels, and from simple gathered headings to tabs and ties. Regardless of your decorating scheme or window, you're sure to find a curtain style that's both practical and beautiful.

By definition, curtains are either gathered on a rod or attached to a rod by tabs, rings, or ties. If the curtains open and close, it's by hand.

LENGTH. Curtain length is variable, depending on the size and shape of the window, the look you want to achieve, and your furnishings. Short curtains that generally cover only the lower half of a window are referred to as café curtains. Refreshingly simple, they're a good choice when you want to show off attractive window frames. Lace or semisheer cafés, with scalloped or gathered headings, are especially nice in a bay, on their own or teamed with shades.

At the other extreme are full-length curtains, which lend themselves to both elegant and informal settings. Extra-long curtains that puddle on the floor impart a luxurious mood; in contrast, simple floor-length curtains tied back high create a casual effect. Bishop's sleeve curtains, one of the more formal styles, consist of long side panels tied back once or twice and then poufed for a classic look.

HEADINGS. Curtains allow for a variety of headings, from gathered to flat.

■ *Rod pocket* is the most common heading treatment. The curtains have a stitched pocket at the top that's gathered, or shirred, onto a rod. If the pocket begins slightly below the top of the heading, a ruffle forms as the curtain is gathered. Extra-wide curtain rods or a pair of rods make possible fuller, deeper headings. When a rod-pocket curtain is gathered at both the top and the bottom, it's called a sash or hourglass curtain.

Extra-long café curtains unify adjoining corner windows of this bath. Knots replace pleats and loop around an attractive brass rod.

Awash in sunshine yellow and floral hues, gathered rod-pocket curtains and coordinating valances share the same fluted rod. Jumbo white welt finishes the edges.

The simplest rod-pocket curtain consists of a single panel pulled back to one side. Ruffled Priscilla curtains that crisscross or meet at the center are a traditional favorite; on a wide window, the curtains may be separated, with the middle portion of the rod covered by a gathered fabric sleeve. Even a seemingly complex treatment of stationary gathered panels topped by an elaborate valance or cornice is just another variation on the basic rod-pocket curtain.

■ **Tab curtains** make a neat, tailored alternative to the rod-pocket style. Matching or contrasting tabs sewn to the top of each curtain panel slip easily over a decorative rod, creating gentle folds. This style naturally goes formal when the fabric is rich.

■ **Rings, bows, or knots** at the top of curtains lend a lighthearted touch. Rings, stitched to the headings and then threaded on a rod, make it easy to open and close the curtains; when fabric is tied or knotted on the rod, the curtains may not move as readily.

LININGS. Linings increase the life of the curtains, reduce noise, block light, and add insulation. When curtains are lined, they have more body and hang better than unlined ones. They also look better because in most cases, the hems don't show from the front.

SHEET SMART

Sheets are naturals for quick-and-easy window treatments. Available in a dizzying array of colors and patterns, from florals to sophisticated designer creations, sheets fit nearly any decorating scheme. And because many sheets have companion patterns, they are a foolproof way to mix designs throughout a room for a coordinated look.

Before you choose a color, design, or treatment style, you'll need to decide which sheets to buy, muslin or percale. Muslin sheets, typically 130 threads per square inch, are less costly than percale but lose their body with repeated washings. Percale sheets, which have from 180 to 250 threads per square inch, are softer and smoother than muslin; they also retain their look and body longer.

To reduce the need for cutting and hemming, work with the dimensions of the sheets as much as possible. Use the top hem for a rod pocket on curtains or a cloud shade; add another row of stitching just below the top edge to create a ruffled heading. If a sheet has an attached border, remove it and turn it into distinctive tiebacks.

Be inventive in hanging the sheets. If the sheet has vertical stripes, hang it from tabs whose stripes run horizontally. Or attach rings, ties, or grommets to the sheet and hang it from hooks or dowels.

Curtain with ties

Swag, cascades & poufs

DRAPERIES

Draperies used to be staid and predictable: pleated panels hanging from hooks attached to narrow traverse rods. But not anymore. A wealth of trims, new choices in hardware and fabrics, and imaginative applications of drapery headings have enlivened this traditional window covering, making possible intriguing, even surprising, window looks.

Draperies dress windows in soft folds of fabric. How those folds fall depends on the fabric, the heading, and whether or not the draperies are lined.

FABRIC CHOICES. The choices in drapery fabrics are many, so many that the decision-making process can be daunting. Try to focus on your practical and decorating needs as you consider the myriad choices.

Sheer fabrics filter daylight and give some daytime privacy, but at night you may want something heavier. That's why sheers are often used as a soft undertreatment with an opaque drapery fabric. Casement fabrics are lightweight, open-weave fabrics traditionally used for draperies; like sheers, they soften a window but generally give greater privacy at night. Medium-weight and heavy fabrics lend a formal, classic look and provide good insulation, light control, and nighttime privacy.

HEADING STYLES. The decor of your room and whether or not you want to add a cornice or valance will probably suggest the best heading style for your

Classic bell valance and drapery treatment evokes an old-world look when made of linen. Rich burgundy borders accentuate the leading edges.

draperies. The pleated styles described below give a consistent appearance, an advantage if you want a formal, traditional window treatment or one that serves as a quiet backdrop for furnishings. When it comes to spacing and depth of pleats, draperies are very flexible: they fit any window and you can specify the pleat size.

■ *French pleats* far outrank all other heading styles in popularity. A French pleat consists of three shallow folds of fabric tacked at the base, repeated at intervals across the entire panel. Pinch pleats are similar to French pleats, except that the folds in the heading are more defined.

■ *Shirred headings* consist of tight little gathers of fabric that fall into soft folds, creating an interesting overall texture. Pleater tape with horizontal rows of cords is sewn to the back of a heading; the cords are then drawn to form gathers. Lighter-weight fabrics are most suitable for this style.

■ *Smocked headings,* a variation of shirred, start out the same but are hand smocked in patterns on the front of the heading. Their softness makes them appropriate for romantic or casual settings.

■ *Box pleats* and inverted box pleats tend to look structured and neat, so they're suitable for formal or tailored interiors.

Shirred headings on both the shaped valance and the draperies underneath produce full, gentle folds in a floral chintz fabric.

■ *Goblet pleats* are the most elegant and elaborate of the pleated headings. For each pleat, a loop of fabric is cinched at the base, forming a goblet shape. Because opening and closing the draperies would crush the pleats, goblet-pleated draperies are always stationary. Rich, deeply textured fabrics lend themselves to goblet pleats.

LININGS AND INTERLININGS. Lining drapery fabric helps protect against fading, adds insulation, and makes the draperies look fuller and hang better. Because the linings are often joined to the hems of the fabric, no stitching shows on the outside of the draperies. An interlining sandwiched between the drapery fabric and lining provides even more insulation.

DECORATIVE DETAILS

When it comes to trimming window treatments, such details as tiebacks, fringe, braid, and ruffles can turn an ordinary curtain, drapery, or shade into something special.

Tiebacks. Whether made of a matching fabric or some other material, tiebacks neatly hold curtains or draperies off the window. Fabric tiebacks, straight, tapered, or scalloped, visually shape and unify the window treatment; you can dress them up with rosettes or bows, if you like. Use cords and rope, with or without tassels, to tie back formal window treatments; braided fabric tiebacks and shirred fabric on jumbo cord are alternatives to traditional cord or rope. Metal or wood holdbacks and medallions elegantly scoop the fabric back from the window.

Usually, tiebacks are placed between a half and a third of the way from the bottom or top of the window. Low tiebacks are generally more formal, high ones more casual. But because their position can affect the amount of light that enters the room, it's a good idea to experiment first with lengths of ribbon tied around the curtain.

Passementerie. Passementerie, a fancy edging or trim, emphasizes the shape and form of curtains, draperies, and shades. Fringe, used on the leading or bottom edges of a treatment, lends rich texture; select a type—cut, loop, tassel, ball, or bullion—that's in keeping with the fabric.

Flat borders and braid define the edges of curtains and Roman shades. Gathered or pleated ruffles made of the same or a contrasting fabric add a romantic touch to curtains and cloud shades. Contrasting or same-fabric welt defines the edges of valances and pelmets.

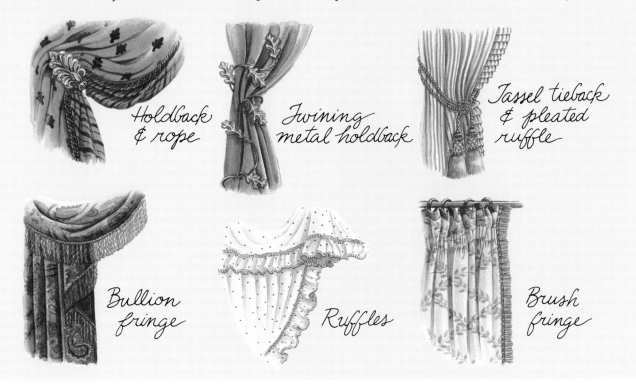

Holdback & rope

Twining metal holdback

Tassel tieback & pleated ruffle

Bullion fringe

Ruffles

Brush fringe

Deep cased windows are finished with flat Roman shades in rich tones that suit the tailored sophistication of this study.

ARCHITECT: JOHN ALLISON, AIA

Outside-mount balloon shades in a classic dot design lend grace and visual interest, and help bring a recessed window forward.

SHADES

From tailored roller and Roman styles to frothy Austrian and balloon creations, shades are as versatile as they are varied.

They're functional too—they provide privacy, block light, and conserve energy. Use them as handsome treatments on their own or coordinate them with other window coverings.

ROMAN SHADES combine simplicity and sophistication in a practical, hardworking window treatment. These classic shades draw up from the bottom by means of cords threaded through rings on the back. When the shade is raised, horizontal folds form, one on top of the other. When down, the shade goes flat, covering the window.

Roman shades can be mounted inside or outside the window frame. An inside mount won't conceal an interesting window frame and allows the lowered shade to hang flush with the wall; an outside mount has the advantage of partially stacking off the glass.

When choosing a fabric for Roman shades, consider how the pattern will look when the shade is drawn up. Some large-scale designs can be jarring when folded up; solid colors and small-scale designs are visually pleasing, folded or flat.

Trims such as braid, gimp, and bands of fabric enhance the strong lines of these good-looking shades.

AUSTRIAN SHADES, like Roman ones, move up and down by means of cords and rings. But vertical shirring on Austrian shades transforms the folds of a Roman shade into soft, draping scallops.

Solid-colored or textured fabrics display the structure of an Austrian shade better than fabrics with busy patterns. Whether patterned or plain, crisp fabrics look more sculptured; sheer or lightweight fabrics accentuate the vertical gathers.

BALLOON AND CLOUD SHADES billow into poufs along the bottom edge when the shade is raised. Strictly speaking, a balloon shade has widely spaced inverted pleats from top to bottom; a cloud shade has a softly gathered heading.

Tailed balloon or cloud shades result when the cords and rings are left off the side edges so that the bottom corners hang below the scallops.

Firmly woven fabrics with vertical stripes complement the structure of balloon shades. Cloud shades, with their gentle gathers, may be made in a crisp or supple fabric, depending on the look you want.

Simple matchstick shades echo the natural texture and warmth of the surrounding woodwork. Light shining through the open weave takes on a luminous quality.

ROLLER SHADES, one of the simplest and most unobtrusive window treatments, let in maximum light when up and neatly cover the entire window when pulled down. On their own, roller shades are suited to small windows and contemporary interiors, decorating situations that require clean design and functionality. Combined with curtains, top treatments, or even other shades, roller shades allow light control and privacy not always possible with soft fabric treatments alone.

Most roller shades are made of vinyl or of stiffened or laminated fabric. Fringe, gimp, braid, and scalloped bottom edges make possible a wide variety of decorative effects.

Conventional-roll shades roll from the back, with the roller in front of the shade; reverse-roll shades roll from the front. Bottom-up shades are mounted on the window sill and are raised rather than lowered.

PLEATED SHADES combine the softness of fabric with the clean lines of a shade. Generally made of permanently pleated polyester fabric, these shades can be sheer (for an unobstructed view), translucent (for glare control and daytime privacy), or opaque (for nighttime privacy and room darkening). Optional metallic backings cut solar gain in summer and reduce heat loss in winter.

Plain pleated shades have simple accordion pleats. Cellular shades consist of two or more layers of fabric attached so that a series of connected cells form when the shades are lowered, creating small,

insulating air spaces. When seen from the side, these shades resemble a honeycomb, a word often used to describe them.

Plain and cellular pleated shades can be made in a fan shape to fit such hard-to-cover areas as circles and arches. Some types even operate from the bottom up, or from the top down and bottom up at the same time.

WOVEN WOOD SHADES are made of thin strips of wood woven together with yarn. Practical and durable, most are Roman shades, some are roll-ups. They can have plain headings or integral valances. Sometimes used alone, woven woods are most often layered under curtains and draperies.

HANDWOVEN SHADES made of natural grasses and reeds bring subtle color, texture, and pattern to windows. Although they provide some daytime privacy, their main functional contribution is the diffusion of light. Use them alone for a simple, airy effect or layer them under fabric treatments for more complete coverage.

ROLL-UP SHADES of fabric, paper, or thin strips of bamboo roll up from the bottom by means of cords and pulleys. Used to screen or block light, they are well suited to most casual settings.

Outfitted in plain stagecoach shades, these windows stand in crisp counterpoint to the room's pattern mix. The shades are held in place with fabric-covered cord.

A sliding shoji screen in a Japanese-style room allows an unobstructed view when open and lets in diffused light when closed. Shojis are also highly insulating.

SHUTTERS & SCREENS

In many situations, such hard-edged treatments as shutters and screens lend elegance, simplicity, and architectural interest to a room. When closed, solid-panel shutters block all light; louvered shutters, lattice screens, and the delicate Japanese shojis allow varying amounts of light to enter.

SHUTTERS. Made of wood that's stained or painted to complement the room's decor, shutters are hinged to the window frame to allow for easy movement. Opened wide, they let in a maximum of light; closed, they afford privacy and light control. Compared with other treatments, shutters can be costly, but they last forever, through any number of changes in a room's decor.

■ *Louvered shutters* allow you to control the amount and direction of light. They also provide privacy, ventilation, and insulation in much the same way as blinds.

Louvers come in a variety of widths, from 1¼ to 4½ inches. Narrow-louver shutters are traditional favorites, but their 1¼-inch louvers obscure the view and block the flow of air.

Wide-louver, or plantation, shutters originated in the South, where they were prized for providing ventilation and sun protection. Their generous louvers mean better insulation and a clearer view.

In addition to covering standard windows, shutters can fold over sliding glass doors and cover such out-of-the-ordinary shapes as arched and cathedral windows.

■ *Solid-panel shutters* make handsome, sturdy window treatments. The panels can be flat, raised, or carved in period designs. They provide complete privacy and good insulation when closed.

SCREENS. Most screens today are made of wood frames with inserts of lattice, cane, or, in the case of shojis, paper or fiberglass. Screens have a clean, uncomplicated look, and they can be used to cover almost any style of window.

Although still made using timeless Japanese methods and materials, shoji screens are being reinterpreted in contemporary materials that are durable and easy to maintain. Rice or mulberry paper is the traditional glazing material; today, thin fiberglass or plastic sheets have replaced the paper in some shojis, making them more practical in rooms that receive moderate to heavy use.

Most often used over sliding glass doors, shoji screens either slide in a track above the door or, when hinged, fold open like shutters. While they preserve privacy, they allow soft, translucent light to enter the room, creating a feeling of spaciousness.

The lines of shoji screens can affect the perceived proportions of a room. Shojis with strong, horizontal grids visually widen and enlarge space; vertical patterns create the illusion of height.

Crisp, clean plantation shutters have extra-wide louvers that, when open, allow good ventilation. The lines of the louvers echo the stripes in the fabric.

Clean lines are the unifying element in a room with an Art Deco theme. Vinyl vertical blinds balance the strong horizontals of the transom window.

BLINDS

Although they differ in appearance, all blinds have slats that compactly stack up or off the window's glazing. The slats themselves tilt for privacy and light control.

With their sleek, hard-edged appearance, blinds are appropriate in most contemporary schemes. But blinds don't absorb much sound, and, with inside mounts, complete darkening may not be possible.

HORIZONTAL BLINDS are practical, versatile window treatments most often defined by the width of their slats.

■ *Venetian blinds,* the original horizontal blinds, have 2-inch-wide slats held together by 1-inch-wide matching or contrasting cotton tapes or nylon cords. Out of style for many years, Venetian blinds are making a comeback in decorating schemes that call for strong, structured window treatments. Their main disadvantage is practical: the wide slats and tapes can be difficult to clean.

■ *Miniblinds,* an updated, pared-down version of Venetian blinds, have 1-inch metal or vinyl slats that tilt when a wand is turned. By far the most popular of all the blinds, they're a good solution if you need intermittent privacy but also want the option of light control and a nearly unobstructed view. Although their clean lines suggest contemporary schemes, miniblinds combine easily with fabric treatments for a variety of window-softening looks.

Two blinds mounted on a single headrail make it possible to use a sliding glass door without uncovering the entire glazed area. Moreover, minis are durable, easy to install, compact when stacked, and relatively easy to clean.

Miniblinds come in a wide range of colors and patterns. If your aim is a functional, understated treatment, stick with neutral solid colors.

■ *Micro-miniblinds,* with their ½-inch slats, are less noticeable than standard miniblinds. In general, they function as minis do, but, because there are more slats, they're bulkier when stacked up.

■ *Wood blinds* combine the natural warmth of wood with the light and privacy control of blinds. Light-colored wood blinds reflect summer sun; in winter, they're more effective insulators than metal or vinyl ones. At home in both traditional and contemporary settings, wood blinds are very long lasting.

VERTICAL BLINDS have all the advantages of horizontal blinds as well as the side-draw operation of draperies. Their wide slats, also called vanes or louvers, can be made of PVC, fabric, wood, aluminum with a baked enamel finish, or polycarbonate plastic; some slats have grooves for wallpaper or fabric strips to match or complement walls or furnishings. Because of the way they operate, vertical blinds are particularly suitable for sliding doors and angled windows.

Unadorned white wood blinds let the focus fall on furnishings. When it's time for a change, the blinds can become the undertreatment for new window coverings.

VALANCES

Shortened versions of curtains, draperies, and shades, valances soften and complete the tops of windows and window treatments. Their versatility allows for a great variety of effects, from tailored to frilly. As with other treatments, the fabric and heading style define the look.

Valances usually repeat, in fabric and form, the treatments they top. But where less than complete coverage is desired to show off windows or let in more light, valances can stand alone. Use them also to cover the headings and hardware of treatments below or to finish treatments that normally have no headings.

GATHERED VALANCES, the most common of all the top treatments, can be formal or casual, depending on their shape and fabric. The simplest valance is made by gathering a fabric sleeve over an extra-wide rod. A traditional gathered valance consists of a short curtain, usually made to match gathered curtains below.

When ruffled along the bottom edge, a valance is generally casual; a gathered valance shaped along the bottom, however, can convey a formal feeling, especially when made in a rich fabric and trimmed

DESIGNER: EMILY MCDANIEL

Box pleats on this cheerful valance fold back and secure with buttons. Revealed is a coordinating fabric that also forms the ties for the shade and makes slipcovers.

with elegant fringe. To show off a contrasting lining, a valance can extend down the sides to form tails.

BOX-PLEATED VALANCES, either straight or shaped along the bottom edge, produce a trim, tailored look. A variation on the box pleat, a bell valance is a flat valance with widely spaced inverted pleats that are narrow at the top and gradually widen toward the bottom. The look is more elegant than either the gathered or box-pleated valance.

BALLOON, CLOUD, AND AUSTRIAN VALANCES are all shortened forms of the shades (see page 12). Like their longer versions, the shirred cloud and Austrian valances are soft and pretty, especially when trimmed with ruffles or fringe; the inverted-pleat balloon valance looks less fussy. Any of the three can have tails, which result when the sides are left to hang below the bottom-edge scallops.

POUF VALANCES are in a category by themselves. Their light, airy appearance is achieved with two rods, the bottom one placed up and under the valance so the fabric blouses. Since the valance doesn't go up or down, you can keep the poufs fluffy by filling them with tissue paper. A double pouf valance has a third rod that slips through a horizontal pocket stitched in the middle of the valance, resulting in an even softer effect than with a two-rod valance.

DESIGN: PAT DAVIS INTERIORS. WINDOW TREATMENT: DIANA JONES

Simple and sweet, a swag valance caps a small bedroom window. Fabric rosettes gather up the folds on either end; an organdy sash curtain provides privacy.

CORNICES, PELMETS & LAMBREQUINS

Added over the headings of curtains, draperies, or shades, a cornice, pelmet, or lambrequin can transform an understated covering into a grand window treatment.

CORNICES are solid top treatments made of painted or upholstered wood or a fabric-covered foam fascia that snaps onto a special rod. The bottom edge of the cornice can be straight, or, in some cases, shaped to echo motifs in the room.

Cornices serve two very practical purposes: they neatly hide the heading and hardware at the top of a treatment, and they block cold drafts coming from the window.

Decoratively, cornices define windows and add architectural interest to a room. When used on adjacent windows, they unify the room and create a pleasing visual rhythm. Atop curtains or draperies, they also provide an opportunity to display the fabric's design over a flat area. Embellishments for cornice edges include same-fabric skirts, braid, gimp, welt, and fringe.

The one real drawback to a cornice is its permanence: once it's constructed, you can't alter it, even a little. And, because of the labor and materials involved, cornices are considerably more expensive than valances.

PELMETS are a cross between valances and cornices. Made of lined or stiffened ungathered fabric, a pelmet can be gently shaped along the bottom edge, much like a cornice, or cut in intricate designs. The shape and design of the pelmet can be inspired by the fabric, by motifs in the room's furnishings, or by architectural details in the room.

Any of the trims appropriate for cornices—welt, braid, gimp, and fringe—will work on pelmets as well. On pelmets with deeply cut edges that form points, small tassels are a traditional finishing touch. Pelmets can also be quilted for additional body and texture.

LAMBREQUINS are simply elaborate cornices that extend part of the way down the sides of the window or, for a dramatic effect, all the way to the floor. Like cornices, lambrequins can be plain or upholstered.

Although most are very formal, they bring whimsy to a child's room when painted or covered in a playful fabric. Because a lambrequin covers a greater area of the window, it's even more efficient than a cornice at keeping heat in and cold out in winter.

WINDOW TREATMENT: MUFFY HOOK

Perfectly in keeping with the room's traditional furnishings, upholstered cornices trimmed with welt and box-pleated skirts crown stationary curtain panels below.

A scalloped pelmet and tailed Roman shade in the same color as the wall draw attention to the graceful fanlight and handsome moldings.

DESIGN: SHELBY DE QUESADA OF SHELBY CO.

A curvaceous asymmetrical swag and cascade make the most of an off-center window. Hand-embroidered net sheers play a supporting role, lengthening the look and letting in light.

DESIGN AND STYLING: JARINDA S. WIECHMAN

This window treatment is a combination of attractive opposites—earthy burlap panels and elegant Battenberg lace—and it works beautifully.

SWAGS & CASCADES

Among the most impressive of all window treatments, swags and cascades bring distinction and classic form to windows. Although they were once found only in the most opulent settings, today's versions adapt to both formal and informal decorating schemes.

CLASSIC SWAGS AND CASCADES look like flowing lengths of fabric, but they are, in fact, carefully constructed treatments. For a classic swag, the fabric is cut on the bias and then folded and draped so it hangs in a semicircle at the top of the window. Cascades, sometimes called tails, are gathered or crisply pleated lengths that hang at the sides. (Although cascades are often called jabots, a jabot actually resembles a short cascade that's pleated on both edges; it usually hangs between two swags.)

Attached to a mounting board, swags and cascades make dramatic top treatments for draperies or full-length curtains. Used alone, they frame and soften the lines of a window without covering very much of the glazing.

The finished look depends on the type and amount of fabric used. For example, a taffeta swag with many folds will be much more formal than a shallow swag made of soft muslin. Whether a cascade is one piece with the swag or a separate piece, it can range in length from a third of the window to all the way to the floor. Shallow swags are casual and let in more light; they suit the proportions of a smaller window. Deeper, more sophisticated swags cover more of the glass and work best on tall windows.

A single swag with cascades is best on a narrow window. For a wide window, hang two swags that meet at the center or use three swags, either overlapping them in one direction or with the center swag placed over or under the outer ones.

DRAPED SWAGS, a less formal alternative to the classic swag style, begin as unshaped pieces of fabric draped loosely on a pole. How the swag looks depends on how the fabric is draped: it can be "snaked" tightly around the pole, loosely draped to expose a decorative pole, or draped asymmetrically with one side puddled on the floor. If you're considering a draped swag, note that the pole must be long enough so the cascades don't cover the window.

For added effect, you can use a contrasting lining; portions of the lining will show as the fabric winds around the pole or falls at the side of the window. Diagonally tapering the ends of the fabric will form tails, exposing the lining even more.

To create a simple draped swag without a pole, lay a length of fabric loosely over brackets or medallion holdbacks mounted at the top corners of the window. Or pull fabric through rings or special swag holders and then shape it into soft poufs.

TRIMS outline and accentuate the gracefulness of sweeping swags and cascades. A traditional trim for the edges of swags and cascades is fringe; intertwining braid, cord, or fringe bordering a classic or draped swag creates another highly decorative look. For the finishing touch, attach rosettes or bows at one or both corners.

ON-THE-SPOT TOPS

Who says stunning can't be simple? Some very dramatic top treatments are also surprisingly easy to make.

No-sew knot. Those knots you see at the tops of windows are a cinch to make. Fold a narrow strip of fabric (about 45 inches long) around a strip of batting to make a tube and secure the ends with rubber bands. Loosely tie the fabric around your wrist (see below); bring the ends to the other side of your wrist and tie again. Slide the knots off your hand and draw through enough of the remaining lengths to form the center of the knot.

One-piece swag. Begin with a piece of fabric 45 or 54 inches wide; the length should equal the width of the window plus 20 inches. Line the panel or hem the edges. Make two parallel rows of long stitches (or use shirring tape) 10 inches in from either side, starting 8 inches up from the bottom and extending to the top edge, as shown below. Draw the threads or shirring tape cords and secure. Attach the swag and then adjust the folds.

Bow valance. Using 54- or 60-inch fabric, cut a length that's twice the desired finished width of the valance and hem the ends. Fold the piece in half lengthwise, placing the fold at the bottom. Then fold the selvages under and attach five clothespins at points 1–5, as shown at bottom left. Mark points along the bottom edge directly below points 2 and 4; bring those points up and attach them with the clothespins. Clip the clothespins over curtains, spacing them evenly. Glue a bow over each clothespin.

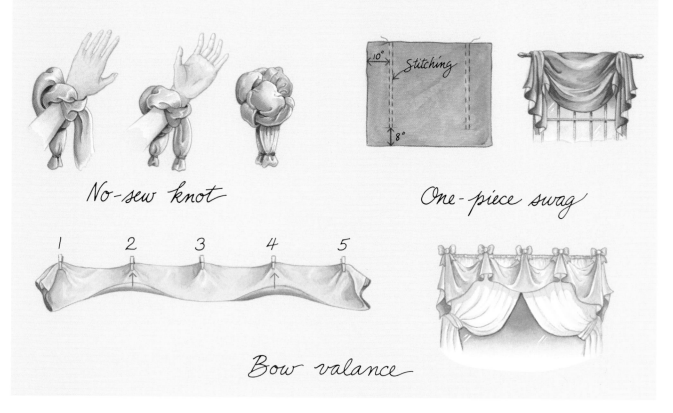

No-sew knot

One-piece swag

Bow valance

WINDOWS & THEIR TREATMENTS

Where would we be without windows? They let in light and air, expand our sense of interior space, and frame our view of the world beyond. But for all their benefits, windows present more than a few problems. Uncovered, they admit harsh sun, passing glances, and chilling drafts. Windows left bare can also appear cold and unfinished unless they're architecturally noteworthy. For both beauty and function, most windows need window treatments.

This section presents 11 basic window styles and suggests successful treatments for each one. If you're building or remodeling, you'll have all kinds of choices; let the ideas and illustrations presented here help you decide which of the many window styles and treatments are best for your home. If, on the other hand, you're dealing with existing windows, the information that follows can provide just the guidance and inspiration you need to make the right decorating decisions.

Some windows are easy to treat; others are more difficult. But almost without exception, you have a wide variety of beautiful and functional treatments from which to choose.

Shutters

Bishop's sleeve curtains

ARCHED WINDOWS

Considered one of the most pleasing window shapes, the arched, or Palladian, window has a long history. Semicircular windows, called fanlights or sunburst windows, were favored in the 1700s, and elliptical fanlights appeared later in the American neoclassical revival. Today's arched windows can be integral or have double-hung or casement windows below a fanlight.

Because the arched window is such a noteworthy architectural element, you may choose to keep it uncovered. Or you can leave the fanlight exposed and treat only the rectangular area below with curtains or shades.

If you want to cover the arched window with a separate curtain, follow the curve with a sheer curtain gathered on a custom-bent rod; where the gathers meet at the center, add a rosette or knot. Sash or tieback curtains below complete the look.

Other treatments that cover both the arched and rectangular portions of the window include bishop's sleeve curtains, a pleated shade with a stationary fanlight shade, and custom shutters that follow the shape of the arch.

Another solution is simply to hang a draped or fabric-wrapped pole above the arch.

AWNING WINDOWS

Like casement windows (see page 22), awning windows are hinged and swing outward. But awning windows are hinged on the top, not on the side, and they're usually small and rectangular.

Awning windows come in a number of possible configurations, all of which give good ventilation. They may occur in stacked pairs or be placed horizontally above or below a fixed window. When grouped horizontally high on a wall, awning windows can take advantage of breezes and light, and, at the same time, maintain privacy.

You have few restrictions when choosing treatments for awning windows. Treatments that clear the glass offer the best ventilation. Shades and blinds that stack up compactly are good choices; so are curtains, draperies, and vertical blinds that stack back. Most treatments suitable for double-hung windows (see page 24) also work on fixed glass and awning window combinations.

For a clean, contemporary treatment that gives good light and ensures privacy, consider double-glazed awning windows with slender miniblinds or pleated shades sandwiched between the two panes.

Miniblinds

Tab curtains

Stagecoach shades

Formal curtains & shades

BAY & BOW WINDOWS

Graceful and romantic, bays and bows are windows of elegant proportions. By definition, a bay is a recessed window with angled sections; when the sections are set in a gentle curve, the window is called a bow.

Because they jut out from the room, bays and bows create a spacious, airy feeling and provide a sweeping view, visually expanding the interior.

You can dress bays and bows in treatments to suit any decorating scheme, from simple to sophisticated. Individual inside-mount shades and blinds of all kinds put the emphasis on handsome window frames. To soften the lines of hard-edged blinds, top them with a continuous fabric valance.

Curtain treatments for bays and bows run the gamut from lacy cafés to rod-pocket curtains or full-length curtains on rings. Formal, full-length curtains mounted outside a bay or bow window, with separate balloon shades on each section, make a dramatic statement.

Traditional draperies, typically a pair of center-meet panels on a hinged or custom-bent rod, have a place on bays and bows, too. Another option is to install a pair of center-meet panels on the middle window and one-way panels on the side windows.

CASEMENT WINDOWS

Hung singly or in pairs, casement windows have sashes that are hinged on the side and swing outward. In a pair, only one window may be operable while the other is stationary, or both may open. Casement windows often flank a fixed glass or picture window.

A casement window provides excellent ventilation because the window can be opened all the way, allowing the outward-swinging sash to catch the breeze. To get the best air flow, choose treatments that clear the glass completely.

Shades and blinds with or without a valance work well on casements; they can be mounted inside or outside, depending on whether you want to cover just the window or the entire frame.

Curtains, draperies, and vertical blinds that stack back expose the entire window; adding an inside-mount shade can give partial coverage and good ventilation during daylight hours when the curtains are opened.

For a cozy effect, try rod-pocket curtains tied back close to the sill. The curtains will cover part of the glass, but they won't blow in the breeze when the window is opened.

Fringed roller shade

Cuffed curtains on rings

Vertical blinds

Plantation shutters

CATHEDRAL WINDOWS

Adding drama to high-ceilinged rooms, cathedral windows are usually angled at the top to follow the slope of the roof. The angled portion, made of fixed glass, is often left bare since privacy isn't a problem when windows are placed so high. Moreover, the view of sky and trees is intended to be seen, and untreated windows let in the most natural light.

When a window has a horizontal crosspiece, it's easy to treat the rectangular shape below, leaving the angled area uncovered. Inside-mount Roman shades, pleated shades, miniblinds, and conventional or bottom-up roller shades are all options. Stationary tieback curtains with sheers underneath provide some privacy and glare control; full-length draperies offer complete nighttime privacy.

If you want to cover the entire window, consider vertical blinds on an angled headrail. Fabric shades, pleated shades, and horizontal blinds can also be made with angled headings, but only the portion of the treatment below the angle can be raised or lowered. Plantation shutters can be custom-made to fit the angle, but they're considerably more expensive than shutters that cover just the rectangular area.

CORNER WINDOWS

The two basic types of corner windows are those that meet glass-to-glass and those that have wall space or window framing in between. Your treatment options depend on the way the windows meet and the look you want to achieve.

For windows with little or no space in the corner, you can try one-way draperies or vertical blinds that open from the corner, allowing separate control of each panel. Make sure the coverings stack back completely when opened; otherwise, the windows will appear smaller.

For a tidy look, hang a pair of stationary tieback curtains on each window; shades underneath give privacy and light control. Or treat each window with a single curtain panel tied back to the side.

Because they stack compactly, inside-mount blinds and shades are appropriate. Where wall space is adequate, you can install outside-mount shades or blinds. Bottom-up or top-down/bottom-up shades that fit within the frames are another option.

Top treatments visually unify corner windows. A series of swags, a pelmet, or a continuous valance can be used alone or over stationary panels or simple shades.

Tieback curtains

Lace panel & swag

Tapered valance on a wide rod

Swags & cascades

DORMER WINDOWS

Windows that project through sloping roofs, dormers generally are small in size, let in little light, and have practically no space on the sides. For these reasons, your treatment choices are limited.

Think first about how you use the room. If it's just an attic hideaway that gets occasional daytime use, perhaps you can leave the window untreated. But if the room is a bedroom, you'll want to cover the window for privacy and light control.

What you do with a dormer window also depends on how it operates. On a window that swings in, sash curtains or sash-mounted miniblinds held down by brackets won't interfere with the movement of the window. For a window that swings out, treatments suitable for outward-swinging casement windows (see facing page) will work, provided there's enough space around the window.

The picture-frame effect of dormer windows can be enhanced by any of the following treatments: tieback curtains with or without a roller shade, café or tab curtains, miniblinds, and all types of shades. For curtains, tension rods mounted between the walls of the recess are often the most convenient hardware.

For a very small window, hang lightweight curtains outside the recess and tie them back to maximize the amount of light entering the room.

DOUBLE-HUNG WINDOWS

One of the most popular window styles, double-hung windows have two sashes—an upper, or outside, sash that moves down and a lower, or inside, sash that moves up. Used alone, in pairs, or in groups, these windows have pleasing proportions that allow for almost any treatment.

With a double-hung window, the treatment can begin at the ceiling, under crown molding, or just above the frame; it can end at the sill, cover the apron or a few inches beyond, or extend to the floor.

Shades have the power to dress up double-hung windows or to cover them quietly. Let the architecture or style of the room dictate the style and level of formality. Pleated shades offer clean lines and good light; structured Roman shades are especially handsome on double-hung windows.

Casual curtain treatments include tab, tieback, and café; for an asymmetrical look, tie a single lace panel to one side.

In a more formal scheme, consider full-length curtains that puddle on the floor. Some of the most sophisticated treatments are tieback curtains or draw draperies topped by a valance, cornice, or pelmet. For a truly classic look, choose swags and cascades.

Rod-pocket curtains

Draped swag & pleated shade

Draperies with bell valance

Curtains with pelmet

FIXED GLASS WINDOWS

Used alone or in combination with sliding or swinging windows, fixed glass windows let in lots of light and frame the view. But depending on their size, they can also allow considerable heat loss in winter and heat gain in summer. That's why it's important to consider energy efficiency (see pages 30–31) when choosing a window treatment for a fixed glass window.

Because they're meant to frame the view, fixed glass windows are usually treated in a way that leaves the glass bare when the treatment is fully opened. Clearing the glass is even more important if casement or sliding windows flank a fixed center window. Full-length curtains or draperies, vertical blinds, and shutters that stack back completely will provide a clear view and balance the large window area. With fabric treatments, you can leave some of the stackback on the window if the view is not outstanding.

Keep top treatments on fixed glass windows simple and light. A deep valance across the top of a large window will only accentuate the width; a loosely draped pole, however, can soften the strong lines.

Where there are no operating side windows, you can also install a bottom-up roller shade or top-down/bottom-up pleated shade in the frame itself.

FRENCH DOORS

Everyone loves French doors. Gracious and charming, they lend character to a room and bring a bit of the outdoors inside. Usually, they consist of a pair of matching doors, one or both of which open inward or outward. With French doors that open outward, you have many options. When they open in, however, any treatment must clear the frame or be attached to the doors themselves.

Lace or sheer sash curtains are a classic French door treatment; however, they will block the light and view. Hourglass curtains, which are like sash curtains but are cinched at the center, allow more light. Blinds, shutters, and pleated or Roman shades are other possibilities, but keep in mind that they will obscure the beauty of the doors.

Formal French door treatments include draperies that stack back completely, topped by a valance, cornice, or pelmet; rod-pocket curtains that puddle on the floor, perhaps with a fabric-covered rod; curtains on rings; and classic swags and cascades.

French doors are occasionally flanked by matching vertical windows (sidelights). You can treat the entire window area as one unit or cover each section separately with blinds, sash curtains, or shades.

Miniblinds

Full-length curtains on rings

Roman shades with cornice

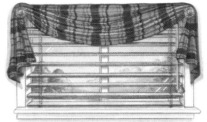

Wood blinds & scarf valance

SLIDING GLASS WINDOWS & DOORS

Composed of two, three, or even four panels, sliding glass windows and doors allow for good ventilation; for this reason, easy operation should be a primary consideration when you're choosing a treatment.

Draperies on one-way traverse rods allow for easy opening of sliders but require a relatively large stacking area; you may decide to keep some of the stackback on the glass of the fixed portion.

Most treatments suitable for casement (see page 22) or double-hung (see facing page) windows work for sliders, provided the window isn't too wide. Treatments should stack back or up to allow for good ventilation. Tieback curtains are traditional. A valance used over shades softens the window's lines.

Vertical blinds are ideal for sliding doors because they stack back completely to allow passage without uncovering the entire door. Other treatments include a pair of blinds or shades on a single headrail; though they stack up compactly, blinds and shades must be raised before you can use the door.

Where you're not concerned about privacy but you want lots of light, consider a draped swag or a pole loosely wrapped with fabric.

Sometimes the best way to set off an arched window is to ignore the arch. This soft, draped shade covers most of the window, but exposes a graceful half-round above.

WINDOW TREATMENT: MARTI CAIRES, MARTHA'S SEWING WORKROOM

Gracefully following the lines of this unusual arched window, a gathered valance tops stationary curtain panels that clear the glass for plenty of light.

NOT-SO-BASIC WINDOWS

What do you do when your windows are a bit out of the ordinary? The solutions can be surprisingly simple.

CLERESTORY WINDOWS, also known as ribbon windows, run along the top of a wall near the ceiling. They're ideal for admitting natural light and heat deep into a room without sacrificing privacy. For these reasons, they're often left untreated.

If you decide to cover clerestory windows, keep the treatment simple and functional. Sill-length curtains or center-draw draperies work well. So do pleated shades, blinds, and shutters. To let in the most light, the treatment should stack back or above completely. Make sure the hardware needed to open or close the covering is easily reachable.

GEOMETRIC WINDOWS often need no treatment at all, especially if they're small squares or trapezoids set high in a wall.

A gathered fabric curtain with a rosette or knot at the center accentuates the shape of a round window; pleated fabric shades can be fanned to fit round, demi-round, or quarter-round windows. Custom miniblinds or screens are another option for round and other odd-shaped windows.

Geometric windows of stained or etched glass are wonderful decorative accents that let in light while ensuring privacy.

GREENHOUSE WINDOWS are baylike windows that project from the house and are designed to fit into existing window openings.

Leave a small kitchen greenhouse window uncovered by day for good air circulation but covered at night, if desired, for privacy. Horizontal and vertical blinds allow good air flow; roller and pleated shades are also possibilities. Just remember to open the treatment in the morning, or the space will quickly get too hot.

A large glass section may require shading to control unwanted heat gain and insulate against heat loss. Consider blinds or Roman, pleated, or quilted shades in tracks that follow the curve of the windows and keep the treatment from sagging.

HOPPER WINDOWS pivot at the bottom and open inward, just the reverse of awning windows. They're most often placed high in basement walls to let in maximum light. Because hopper windows open inward, any treatment must clear the glass completely.

Curtains on rings or simple draw draperies are practical choices, as are shades or blinds mounted above the frame. Sash curtains attached to the frame allow easy opening and closing of the window.

SIDELIGHTS AND TRANSOMS bring welcome light to an entry. Sidelights are the thin vertical windows that flank a door. A transom is a window above a door. When a transom is arched, it's referred to as a fanlight or sunburst window; shallow arches are called eyebrows.

Since they're intended to bring in natural light, sidelights and transoms are often left untreated. For privacy, lace or sheer sash curtains are traditional on sidelights, but miniblinds and microminis will also give light in the day and privacy at night.

SKYLIGHTS let natural light stream in, bringing warmth deep into a room without any loss of privacy. But when there's too much light, glare, or heat loss, skylights need to be covered. Pleated shades, miniblinds, and quilted fabric shades are all effective. Most treatments can be motorized and programmed to open and close based on the amount of light and heat coming into the room.

Roman shades on guide wires open and close over skylights, allowing full sun or filtered light. Such flexible light control makes the sun space usable throughout the day.

WINDOW SEATS

Dress a window seat with a special window treatment and you'll want to linger longer, to read or just to enjoy the view.

To frame a window seat, hang curtains or draperies outside the recessed window. Curtains that open and close on rings are simple and casual; draperies topped by a pleated or gathered valance create a more sophisticated look. To cover the alcove just a bit, hang stationary rod-pocket curtains outside the window seat and tie them back low, near seat height.

Choose an inside-mount treatment when you want to cover just the window and not the entire window seat area. Cloud and balloon shades are fluffy and romantic, blinds and Roman shades more tailored. For a window seat that's also a bay, unify individual inside-mount treatments with a top treatment. Used alone, a continuous pouf valance softens a window seat while allowing plenty of light to enter.

Whatever treatment you choose, you can pull the look together with matching or coordinating pillows and cushions. Just remember that if the view is outstanding and privacy and light control are not concerns, this is a wonderful window to leave bare.

Draperies with valance

Tieback curtains

Cloud valance

PUTTING IT ALL TOGETHER

Although you may not be able to change the style of your windows unless you're building or remodeling, you can easily change your window treatments. Often, modifying what's covering your windows can dramatically affect the appearance of a room, bringing in more light, opening up the room to the out-of-doors, adding pattern and texture. But how do you know what treatment style, shape, or color is best for your particular situation? Here's help.

FUNCTIONAL CONSIDERATIONS

It's obvious: windows are designed to admit light. But windows play a myriad of other roles, ranging from purely decorative to hardworking. Understanding how windows and their coverings function can help guide you to window treatments that both express your style and meet your needs.

LIGHT. Providing natural light *is* the primary function of windows. In fact, "lots of light" is a wish frequently expressed by people who are planning new construction or a remodel. Light gives life to a room, creating a mood, enhancing colors, and revealing textures. How much light actually enters a room depends on many factors: the number of windows; their size, shape, and location in the wall; buildings or shrubbery outdoors; and the color of the room's furnishings, walls, floor, and ceiling.

If your goal is to admit the maximum amount of light into the room, you'll want to choose a window covering that completely clears the window glass, at least during daylight hours. To filter the light and control glare, your choices include sheer and semisheer curtains and draperies, translucent pleated shades, and shoji screens. Some light-filtering materials, such as lace, create interesting textural patterns when light comes through them.

The most effective light-blocking treatments are lined curtains, draperies, or shades, especially those with blackout linings. Blinds of all kinds, when tilted, block most of the light, as do louvered shutters.

When you're considering light control, don't forget the sun's potential to damage fabrics and furnishings. Lined window treatments will last longer than unlined ones; they'll also protect the room's furnishings better. Even a translucent undertreatment can help block some of the sun's destructive rays.

CLIMATE. There's nothing like a breeze blowing through an open window to cool and freshen your home. But not every window provides the same amount of ventilation. Side- and top-hinged windows, such as casement and awning types, let in the most air because they open fully; double-hung and sliding windows are less efficient because only half the window area can be exposed to air flow. Open windows on opposite sides of a room provide the best cross-ventilation.

To take advantage of the cooling effects of windows, be sure that your window coverings don't get in the way of the breeze. Billowing curtains not only block air flow but also are visually distracting.

You can't consider climate control and windows without taking into account the importance of solar gain and heat loss. Solar gain is the heat that passes through windows and is absorbed in the room. It's a plus when you use that heat to augment your heating system, but it's undesirable when you want the interior to stay cool in summer. In cold-winter regions, you'll want to reduce heat loss through windows as much as possible. For details on how window coverings can affect heat gain and loss, see pages 30–31.

When lowered, opaque pleated shades admit soft light; raised, they nearly disappear from view. Either way, they don't detract from the room's decorative elements.

Striped Roman shade underneath a flowing one-way curtain provides privacy, as well as light control and insulation.

PRIVACY. Any window in your home has the potential for allowing people to see inside. In some rooms, that may not be a concern. But where it matters, sheers and lightweight fabrics can let some light through while at the same time offering daytime privacy. At night, you'll need stronger treatment, such as lined draperies that close completely or opaque shades, louvered shutters, or miniblinds.

NOISE CONTROL. Open or closed, windows allow noise to penetrate into a room. But window coverings can reduce noise, whether it's coming from outside or inside the house. In general, the softer and more generous the treatment, the more it will absorb sound. Soft fabric treatments reduce noise the most; pleated shades muffle sound somewhat, especially when used under a fabric treatment.

VIEW. When a large window frames a magnificent view, that view is likely to become the focal point of the room. Even if the view encompasses just a few trees or a small garden, it may be worth preserving.

When the view deserves to be seen, choose a treatment that clears the glass completely during the day. Curtains and draperies that pull back are obvious solutions; blinds and shades that stack up work just as well. Windows with great views are not the place for low-draping tieback curtains or heavy top treatments that obstruct the view. A treatment that repeats the color and pattern on the wall will not distract the eye from the view beyond.

But when the view is forgettable or unattractive, the window treatment itself can command attention. Fabrics with intriguing colors and patterns provide more interest than plain fabrics. Combination treatments—curtains with a shade, for example—put the focus on the window, not on the view.

For a view you never want to see, install shutters, blinds, or translucent shades that block the view but still let in some light.

BRINGING THE OUTDOORS INSIDE. When you're inside, windows are an important connection to the outside world. Large windows seem to enlarge interior space and make the outside a visual extension of a room; even smaller windows have an expansive effect. French or sliding glass doors open the interior and allow indoor living to flow outdoors easily and conveniently. Windows and doors bring the color and fragrance of the garden into your home; seasonal color can be planned to enhance a room's decor.

Minimal window treatments, such as a simple curtain or softly draped swag, strengthen the visual link between interior and exterior spaces.

Dramatic and functional, wide-louver plantation shutters let the sun stream in or tilt for privacy. Offset tilt bars make it possible to adjust the louvers on all the windows.

ENERGY SAVERS

Window treatments can do more than simply decorate a window. Some are designed to shade the interior from the sun; others help retain warmth in winter. More than a few are intended to provide year-round insulation against both heat and cold. Although no treatment can do everything, the challenge is to select one that both looks great *and* saves energy.

As you think about energy efficiency, keep in mind that most window treatments, even those not designed as energy savers, will have an insulating effect.

Energy lingo. Understanding such terms as conduction, convection, radiation, and R and U values will help you shop for energy-efficient windows and window treatments.

■ *Conduction* occurs when heat passes from one object to another. Heat passes quite readily through ordinary glass, steel, and aluminum. But window frames made of wood, vinyl, or fiberglass are poor conductors, so less heat is lost.

■ *Convection* is movement of air that carries heat from warmer surfaces to cool ones. When warm room air moves toward a cold window and hits the glass, the air is cooled and sinks to the floor, allowing more warm air to come in contact with the glass. This cooling convective current can be interrupted by a window treatment that acts as an insulating barrier.

■ *Radiation* is the transmission of heat from the sun. The heat is either reflected by the glass or passes through the glass and is absorbed by objects. The absorbed heat is then reradiated, but some remains inside the room, creating a greenhouse effect.

To reduce radiation loss in winter and radiation gain in summer, you'll need a window treatment that keeps the heat from leaving or entering the room. Glass, films, and screens can also play an important role; for more information, see pages 76–77.

■ *R value and U value* are terms related to heat loss. R value measures a material's ability to resist heat flow; the higher the number, the more energy efficient the material. Many window treatments are assigned R values, but the treatment must be used properly and consistently to realize energy savings.

U value measures a material's ability to conduct heat; the lower the number, the more energy efficient the material. U values are most often assigned to windows rather than window treatments. They mea-sure the rate of heat flow through the entire window, not just through the glass or through the frame. For more on U values, see page 73.

Reducing excessive heat gain. In summer, excessive heat gain can be a problem, especially in rooms that face south or west. The most effective way to reduce heat gain is to stop the sun's rays outside, before they get to the glass. Interior treatments allow some heat to enter, but they may be more convenient to use than exterior treatments. Both approaches will, unfortunately, block light and obstruct the view.

Note that some of the strategies for reducing unwanted heat gain in summer can help retain heat in winter. For example, deciduous trees that shade well in summer allow sunlight to warm a house in winter, especially when the room's window treatment completely clears the glass. Also, rolling shutters that guard against summer heat gain defend against heat loss in winter. Even some shades can insulate in winter.

■ *Landscaping* is hardly a window treatment, but it is the first line of defense against heat gain. Trees shade windows and cool the air through the release of moisture. Deciduous trees block the sun's rays in summer.

■ *Awnings* help keep indoor temperatures down by shading windows. The amount of heat reduction depends on the direction the window faces and the color of the awning fabric. Some awnings can be retracted from the inside; others, sensing the sun and wind, open and close automatically.

■ *Louvered shutters* block sun while allowing ventilation, thereby reducing heat gain. Exterior shutters block the light before it hits the glass, but they must be opened and closed from the outside. Interior shutters are easy to adjust by tilting the louvers.

■ *Rolling shutters,* long favored in Europe, consist of interlocking horizontal slats made of aluminum or PVC. The aluminum slats are filled with foam insulation; the PVC slats have a honeycomb structure that creates insulating air spaces. Both kinds of shutters protect against heat gain.

■ *Shades,* either plain pleated or cellular pleated, with light-colored or metallic backings reduce heat gain. Even roller shades provide some insulation. For curved glass sections and skylights, consider quilted insulating shades in tracks.

■ **Blinds,** both horizontal and vertical, with white or reflective backings bounce incoming heat back out the window. Light-colored wood blinds are also good at reducing unwanted heat gain.

■ **Solar screens** effectively reduce heat gain by shading windows. Exterior screens that keep the sun from hitting windows offer the best protection. Lightweight screens of woven fiberglass mesh block the sun but allow breezes to enter. Heavier screens of vinyl-coated polyester fabric are best on windows where the sun is constant. For even more protection, choose louvered aluminum shade screens.

Interior screens, opaque or semisheer, are somewhat less effective, but they're practical because they're easily raised and lowered from the inside. Soft screening materials can be made as draperies, vertical blinds, or roll-up, Roman, or pleated shades.

Preventing heat loss. A number of energy-saving treatments and strategies can keep the interior of your home warmer in winter.

■ **Multilayered or combined treatments** insulate windows and inhibit heat loss. Typical examples are curtains with a pleated shade underneath or heavy draperies with sheer draperies next to the glass.

■ **Draperies** that reach from the ceiling to the floor prevent the heat loss that can occur when the treatment starts only at the top of the window. Making a treatment wider than the window also impedes convective currents.

■ **Linings** can greatly increase the energy efficiency of curtains, draperies, and shades. In addition to linings made of standard cotton and cotton-polyester blends, you can order energy-efficient insulating and/or blackout linings. Interlinings provide even more insulation.

■ **Edge sealing** involves attaching the treatment to the window frame or wall to impede the flow of air to and from the glass. Edge-sealing treatments are more important on older windows that leak; insulating glass (see page 76) found in newer dwellings is more energy efficient.

Flexible magnetic strips (available from some interior designers and through some window treatment workrooms) can be attached to the frame or wall and enclosed in the edge of a curtain, drapery, or soft fabric shade. Hook and loop fastening tape (available at fabric stores) can also be used to seal the edges of a treatment to the wall.

■ **Shades** can sometimes reduce heat loss from convection. Outside-mount shades that cover the frame help prevent air infiltration; inside-mount shades must fit snugly within the frame to be effective. Quilted shades, available as Roman shades, roll-up shades in tracks, or window "blankets" hung with hook and loop fastening tape, are designed to insulate with a vapor barrier and multiple layers of fabric and batting.

■ **Cornices,** painted or upholstered, are poor conductors of heat; because they enclose the top of a treatment, they also block convective currents.

■ **Swags and cascades** or valances attached to mounting boards work in the same way as cornices to block the loss of heat at the top of a treatment.

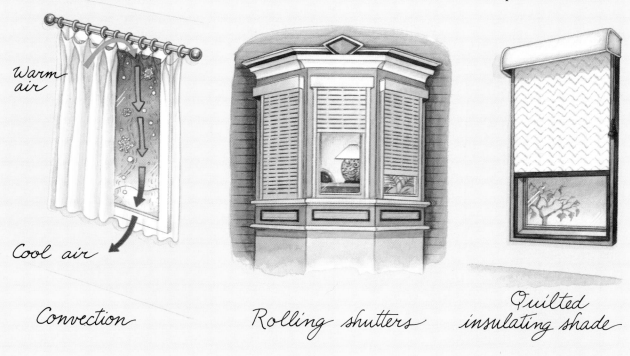

Warm air

Cool air

Convection

Rolling shutters

Quilted insulating shade

DECORATING BASICS

Whether it's the focal point of the room or a quiet backdrop for distinctive furnishings or artwork, a well-planned window treatment combines basic design elements—color, texture, and pattern—in a way that creates a beautiful, balanced effect. Understanding the theory that underlies those design elements will help you achieve just the look you want.

Of course, the style of your home and its furnishings will dictate many of your decisions. For guidelines on choosing appropriate treatments for different windows and decorating schemes, see the individual descriptions beginning on page 8.

COLOR IS PRIMARY. The most powerful design element, color can also be the most confusing for the home decorator. Regardless of the type of window covering you choose, you'll be forced to make some important color decisions. Before you do, it's a good idea to learn some color principles.

■ **Color terms.** *Hue* is just another word for color. Every hue has a "visual temperature." Yellow, red, and orange are warm and lively; they're often referred to as advancing colors because they seem nearer than they are. Blue, green, and violet are cool and tranquil; they're often called receding colors because they appear to be farther away.

Just as important as actual color is *intensity,* the degree of purity, or saturation, of color. Although

Color wheel

both robin's egg blue and indigo are technically blue, for example, they differ in their intensity, or strength, of color. *Value* is the amount of light and dark in a color; color with white added is a *tint,* color plus black a *shade.*

■ **The color wheel.** As you look at the color wheel, at left, remember that most colors used in decorating schemes are altered or combined in ways that soften their impact.

All color combinations and variations come from the color wheel. Although the color wheel can't dictate schemes, it can help you imagine what will happen when colors are put together.

Primary colors—red, blue, and yellow—are the source of all other colors. Primaries are powerful, usually too powerful to use full strength on such large areas as windows.

Secondary colors lie midway between the primary colors on the wheel because they're formed by combining primaries: green comes from blue and yellow, orange from yellow and red, and violet from red and blue. Secondary colors are less strong than primaries.

Intermediate colors result when you mix a primary color with an adjacent secondary color. Blue (a primary) and violet (a secondary) combine to make blue-violet, an intermediate.

Complementary colors are those opposite each other on the wheel. Red and green are complements, as are blue and orange, yellow and violet.

Neutral colors are white, black, and variations of gray. Low-intensity warm colors such as beige and ecru are also considered neutrals and are often used in understated window treatments.

■ **Combining colors.** Your room's decor may already suggest a color scheme, or perhaps you have some favorite colors you want to use in combination. Whatever the case, understanding the three basic types of color schemes will help you devise your own. Again, keep in mind that the colors are usually softened versions of the colors on the wheel.

Monochromatic schemes consist of one color in a variety of intensities and values. Because colors have so much in common in monochromatic schemes, rooms appear unified and harmonious.

Complementary color schemes are those based on colors opposite each other on the color wheel. They tend to be richer than monochromatic schemes because they balance warm and cool colors. These combinations can be startling or subdued: instead of

Garden-fresh colors from all around the color wheel blend harmoniously in a ruffled cloud valance. Coordinating patterns on walls and furnishings unify the look.

expansive, dark colors more intimate and space contracting. To increase the sense of light in a dull room, use pale tints of warm or cool colors on windows and walls. To make a large room seem cozier, use rich, dark shades that draw in the space. Elsewhere in the room, be sure to repeat colors used at the window to pull together and balance the scheme.

Color is also affected by the direction of light. Windows facing south and east let in warm, cheering light. Indirect northern light is softer and cooler, and light from the west is the harshest of all. You can use your awareness of light to guide your color choices. For example, a room facing north will feel more cheerful bathed in warm color, while cool hues tone down the bright light in a west-facing room.

Some additional color thoughts: If the room's scale can handle a window treatment that's bold or brightly colored, fine. But remember that you'll probably be living with the treatment for many years. Low-value, less-intense colors may "wear" better visually than strong ones. Also, keep in mind that when quantities of fabric are gathered, as in draperies, curtains, and some valances, for example, the color will appear intensified.

Neutral doesn't have to mean off-white or beige. The stagecoach window shade is a deep mushroom that is the perfect foil for the dark-green walls, colorful accessories, and wood furniture.

violet and yellow, think about a quiet room with soft amethyst curtains and creamy walls.

Within the complementary category, there are more complex combinations. A *triad* consists of any three colors equidistant on the color wheel. A *split complement* also has three colors—one primary color plus the color on each side of its opposite; yellow plus red-violet and blue-violet is an example of a split complement.

To avoid the clash of pure opposing color, always vary the intensity, quantity, and value of complementary colors. Look carefully at fabrics with complementary schemes to see how colors are varied and balanced. Often, you can start with a well-designed fabric and use its colors to plan your color scheme.

Analogous, or related, color combinations are composed of two or more colors that lie next to each other on the color wheel. This combination results when you start with a favorite color and add related colors to it.

■ *Color's qualities.* Thinking about how colors actually appear will make it easier for you to visualize window treatments. In general, light colors are

THE ROLE OF TEXTURE. Shiny chintz curtains, hard-edged blinds, rich tasseled fringe—all window treatment materials possess texture, from distinctive to subtle. When the texture is smooth, light is reflected and colors appear lighter and more lustrous; smooth materials often appear cool and sophisticated. When there's more texture, the material appears duller because the texture absorbs rather than reflects light. Window treatments with noticeable texture—woven shades and nubby cotton curtains, for example—tend to be casual, though there are exceptions.

How much texture you use on your windows depends, in part, on how you've used color and pattern in the room. A neutral color scheme with very little pattern allows for more texture than a scheme with bold color or pattern. Try to introduce enough texture to create interest, but not so much that visual chaos results. And remember, patterned fabric has a visual texture, too.

PATTERN PANACHE. When to use pattern and how to combine different patterns are perplexing decorating questions. You can develop pattern confidence if you follow some basic pattern principles. There are no hard-and-fast rules, but observing how patterns appear at windows and how they interact when used throughout a room will make the job of selecting and combining patterns easier.

DESIGNER: ELIZABETH POOLE

Color is the tie that binds an array of country patterns, from the florals and checks on bed and bedside table to the blue scrollwork of the sheer Roman shades.

White plantation shutters and cocoa-colored walls illustrate the power of solid color in a decorating scheme. Contrasting textures add visual interest.

■ *Pattern style.* Choose patterns that are in keeping with the style of the room and the windows. For example, a tapestry fabric with an old-world quality looks appropriate covering tall windows in a period room; in a rustic cabin with tiny windows, a small-scale stylized pattern fits right in.

■ *Pattern scale.* The size of a pattern should correspond to the scale of the room and its windows. Small-scale patterns are often used in small rooms, where their design is clearly retained and seen. A large room can support large-scale patterns. Because they seem to contract space, large-scale patterns can create the impression that a room is smaller than it actually is.

■ *Pattern combinations.* Patterns that share at least one color combine naturally; similar patterns of different scales can also be combined. If you choose to place a bold pattern on your windows, add one or two smaller-scale patterns to the room, distributing them so that you avoid pattern clusters.

For decorating purposes, you can approach pattern in three different ways. The first is simplicity—unpatterned walls, windows, and furnishings. The clean Shaker style is an example of beauty achieved through simplicity. Simple can also be formal; for example, softly colored silk taffeta draperies with a tasseled pelmet look elegant against neutral, solid-color walls. When you choose a scheme without obvious pattern, let subtle textures come into play.

Another approach is to use pattern throughout—on the windows, on the walls, even on the furnishings. This all-out mix of patterns can be tricky to pull off successfully, however; think about your choices carefully before you commit to anything. One of the easiest-to-accomplish combinations consists of light and airy patterned walls punctuated by darker, more densely patterned window treatments. Subtle striped walls, for example, can echo bolder stripes in a balloon shade. Or put soft stripes on walls

and a floral treatment on windows, maintaining at least one common color. An alternative is to use the identical pattern on windows and walls, though it's not as common an approach.

A third option is to combine pattern with plain color for a balanced look. Keeping walls plain while dressing windows in pattern is a good way to draw attention to the window and the window treatment. The window treatment itself may be a combination of plain and patterned fabrics—a solid-color cloud shade with a patterned heading and ruffle, for example.

VISUAL EFFECTS

Are your windows too narrow for the size of the room? Do you wish they were a little higher in the wall? Here are some visual "tricks" you can use with different window treatments to affect the apparent size and proportions of your windows.

With blinds and shades, the type of mount you choose makes a difference in the perceived dimensions of the window. An inside-mount blind, for example, emphasizes the actual size of the window; mounted outside, a shade makes the window look a little wider than it is.

Soft fabric treatments offer even more opportunities to fool the eye. Inside-mount sash or tieback

curtains contract the space, making a window look smaller. To create the illusion of height, hang a valance above a window so that the bottom edge of the valance just covers the top of the window. To shorten a tall window, hang the valance so that the top edge just covers the window frame. A full fabric treatment that stacks off the glass almost completely will make a narrow window appear wider, as will a treatment with a strong horizontal element, such as a cornice or valance.

Where you place tiebacks affects window proportions. When curtains or draperies are tied or held back high, the window appears narrower; low tiebacks create the sense of a wider window.

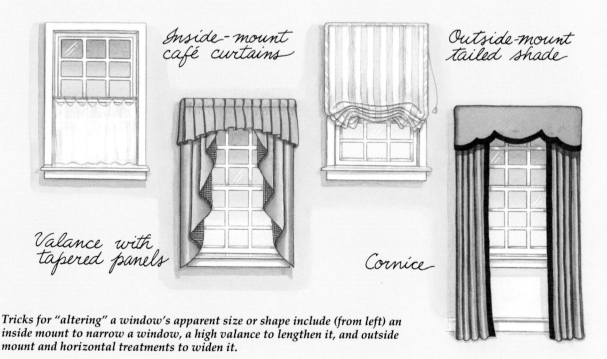

Tricks for "altering" a window's apparent size or shape include (from left) an inside mount to narrow a window, a high valance to lengthen it, and outside mount and horizontal treatments to widen it.

PRACTICAL MATTERS

Will your window treatments have to be custom-made? How much material is required? What will it all cost? You'll need answers to these questions and more before you can make your final decisions.

READY-MADE OR CUSTOM TREATMENT? In some cases, all that stands between you and a finished window is a trip to a home furnishing or department store with a large stock of ready-made window treatments. Armed with exact measurements (see below) and some firm ideas on style and color, you may be able to purchase a suitable window covering right off the shelf.

But often, something custom-made is called for. If you know what you want in both treatment and fabric, you can work with a person who fabricates window treatments. Some home furnishing and fabric stores will sell you the fabric and have it made up for you in their own workrooms.

If you're unsure of exactly what window treatment is right, an interior designer or decorator can help you choose a style and fabric, and can usually recommend a fabricator. The designer will then order the fabric for you and deal directly with the fabricator. Most designers charge by the hour for their time; in addition, you'll have to pay the cost of materials and labor.

After looking at all the options, you may decide that you're up to making your own fabric window treatments. Unless you're experienced, choose a style that won't reveal less-than-perfect sewing skills, such as rod-pocket or tab curtains, a one-piece swag, or a simple gathered valance.

MEASURING WINDOWS. For general information and pricing, it's enough to know the basic size of your window. But if you're taking measurements to order a specific treatment, you must be exact. Here are some guidelines for accurate measuring.

■ Use a steel tape measure (cloth ones stretch) and record all measurements in inches.

■ For inside-mount blinds or shades, measure the width within the frame at the top, center, and bottom, and use the narrowest dimension. For the height, measure within the frame from the soffit to the sill. For ready-made treatments, provide the exact inside window measurements; the manufacturer makes allowances for the treatment to fit inside the frame.

■ Outside-mount treatments can cover just the window frame area, or they can extend beyond the frame onto the walls. Measure the width and height of the frame; then add the distances you want the treatment to cover beyond the frame.

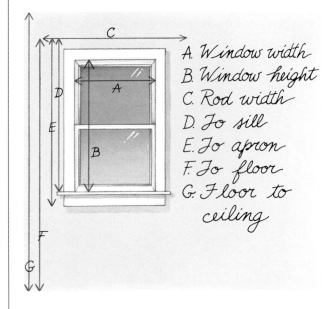

A. Window width
B. Window height
C. Rod width
D. To sill
E. To apron
F. To floor
G. Floor to ceiling

ESTIMATING FABRIC. You can get an idea of the cost of curtains and draperies by estimating the yardage needed. (Don't forget to add the costs of hardware, lining, and trim to the fabric cost.) The general instructions here are for estimating *only*.

1. Measure (in inches) the width of the area the treatment will cover according to the type of mount you've chosen—inside or outside. Measure the desired finished length.

2. Multiply the width times the desired fullness—usually 2½ times for medium-weight or heavy fabrics, 3 times for sheers. Add 3 inches for each side hem. This figure is the total width.

3. Divide the total width by the width of the fabric to get the number of widths needed.

4. Determine the cut length by adding 16 inches (for headings, hems, and a little extra) to the finished length.

5. Multiply the number of fabric widths by the cut length. Divide this figure by 36 to get the number of yards needed.

CONSIDERING COSTS. Costs vary widely, depending on the size of the window, the type of treatment, the materials used, and where the treatment is made. Hard-edged treatments such as miniblinds are usually less expensive than soft fabric ones. Among the most costly treatments are custom-made plantation shutters and elaborate draperies topped with an upholstered cornice.

In general, ready-made treatments are less expensive than custom ones. But don't automatically assume that ready-made treatments are the best buy. Custom work may not cost much more, and the difference in quality can be significant. Start by looking at treatments you like in your price range. Shop carefully and compare prices. For more information on costs, see the chapter beginning on page 71.

A WINDOW TREATMENT QUESTIONNAIRE

A quick glance at the questionnaire below can start the ideas flowing. As you develop your plans, come back to this page often; then you'll be sure that you've chosen a treatment that meets as many of your needs as possible.

Design guidelines

■ What's the style of your home and its furnishings? Often, it will suggest a window treatment style.

■ Is the window distinctive? Perhaps some interesting architectural details deserve emphasis.

■ Are the window's proportions pleasing? If not, try some of the visual tricks described on page 35.

■ Is the view outstanding? If it is, choose a treatment that won't detract from what's outdoors.

■ How much space surrounds the window? Ideally, you should be able to stack treatments off the window. Where space is limited, choose a treatment that stacks compactly.

■ How much coverage do you want? Options range from inside mounts to floor-to-ceiling.

■ How will your window treatments look from the outside? If your home can be viewed from the street, aim for a consistent look at the windows, one that's in keeping with the exterior style of the house.

Practical questions

■ How much privacy do you need? Lace and sheer treatments give some daytime privacy; opaque treatments block the view from outside at night.

■ How much natural light do you want inside the room? For maximum light, choose a treatment that, when open, clears the glass.

■ Do you need to control glare? Sheer and translucent window treatments cut glare while admitting diffused light.

■ Do you need protection against sun damage? A light-diffusing treatment minimizes sun damage. Lining fabric treatments will protect furnishings and fabrics.

■ How much ventilation do you want? Where good ventilation is a priority, choose a window treatment that doesn't block the flow of air.

■ Is noise control a consideration? Lined fabric treatments muffle sound most effectively.

■ Is the window frequently opened and closed? If so, the treatment should not get in the way.

■ What's your life-style? If it's hectic choose durable treatments that are easy to maintain. Save elaborate layered looks for formal rooms.

■ What about your current furnishings? If you plan to live with them for a while, choose a window treatment that works with what you have. If you're planning to redecorate, you may be able to install a simple treatment now, such as a valance or blind, and add to it later on when your budget or schedule allows.

Child safety

■ Are drapery, shade, or blind cords within the reach of babies or young children? Clamp cords to the window covering itself or wrap them around a cleat mounted high on the wall. Shortened cords and wands are available by special order.

■ Can windows be opened enough for a child to fall out? Install window locks that allow only partial opening.

■ Can children climb furniture to reach windows? Move furniture away from the windows to put temptation out of reach.

■ Can young children easily pull on curtains or draperies? A temporary solution is to loop them up, beyond a child's reach. Also, be sure that mounting hardware is securely fastened to the wall.

GREAT WINDOW TREATMENTS

Like a tour through a number of well-designed homes, this collection of window treatments overflows with visual excitement. As you shop these pages for inspiration, you'll see familiar styles as well as innovative ones. Although your windows may not look like those in the photos, many of the treatments are easily translatable.

As you study each photo, ask yourself, What makes this treatment work? Perhaps it's the way the treatment's style enhances the room's decor. Or maybe it's how different coverings combine to produce a treatment that's both practical and good-looking.

And don't overlook the details. A bit of fringe, a faux-painted pole, or a fanciful tassel can turn an everyday treatment into a scene-stealer.

Minimum treatments can have maximum impact, especially when the colors are bright and the patterns bold. Shaped gathered valances trimmed with jumbo welt knotted on the ends and tacked in place let in plenty of light. A parade of pillows makes the window seat even more inviting.

Light-filtering dotted-swiss sheers edged with pink satin ribbon provide the undertreatment for crisp cloud valances. Ruffles and linings on bows are done in a coordinating plaid.

Elaborately ornamented curtains are held back with brass medallions to permit a full view. French pleats decorated with bows attach to rings; ropes and tassels add subtle color and curves.

CURTAIN CALL

DESIGN: CORINNE WILEY, ASID

Fabrics with a rich mix of old-world color and pattern amply dress a bathroom window in an arresting curtain and swag combination. A cabana-stripe swag covers a simple cornice box; edge-softening tiebacks and cascading corner tendrils are fashioned from dried flowers (see detail at right).

DESIGN: JANET DUTKA INTERIOR ARCHITECTURE & DESIGN

CURTAIN
CALL

Neoclassical cuffed curtains take center stage in a sophisticated eclectic scheme. Grecian figures and subtle shades of sage, cream, rust, and teal play against a marbled charcoal background; the folded-over striped lining is definitely meant to be seen. Brass medallions—actually drawer pulls—decorate the heading (see detail at left).

Generous tieback curtains are made of fabric inspired by the style known as chinoiserie. Individual petals cut from faille, a tightly woven fabric with tiny ribs, overlap for a deep, dramatic edging. Silk sheers veil the view.

DESIGN: CHARLEEN MATOZA, LA FILLE DU ROI INTERIORS
WINDOW TREATMENT: C. C. CAHOOTS CUSTOM SEWING

WINDOW TREATMENT: MUFFY HOOK

Framing a see-worthy view with floral hues and patterns, graceful bishop's sleeve curtains show off handsome windows and allow full light. Four-inch ruffles on the curtain panels and shirred sleeves create the impression of one continuous heading.

GREAT WINDOW TREATMENTS **43**

Sheer hourglass and sash curtains on French doors and sidelights lend understated elegance to a formal dining room. The banded hourglass curtains are a classic French-door treatment; rosettes are made from bias-cut lengths of fabric ruffled and then rolled and sewn into flower forms.

DESIGN: MARTI CAIRES, MARTHA'S SEWING WORKROOM

SOFT SOLUTIONS FOR FRENCH DOORS

Windows and doors dressed in the same colorful chintz unify a traditional kitchen. French doors and sidelights sport neat Roman shades with stitched-down folds. The balloon shade is stationary—miniblinds underneath provide light control and privacy when necessary.

Ruffled rod-pocket curtains, tied back high, bare French doors and allow light to stream in. Stylized floral motifs in the fabric mix well with the geometric pattern on the walls and hint at the garden beyond. Antique furniture and colorful accessories add to the European country ambience.

SHADES OF FABRIC

WINDOW TREATMENT: MUFFY HOOK

Muted stripes flow gently down the face of a looped Roman shade; extra fabric between the rings means the folds stay softly rounded, even when the shade is lowered. The whimsical oversized valance is simply a width of fabric attached to a mounting board and drawn up at the center.

Tailored and traditional, outside-mount Roman shades dress windows in quiet colors. The shades draw up by means of rings and cords attached to the back; jaunty tails are the result of leaving the rings off the side edges. A welted cornice conceals the shades when they're raised completely.

ARCHITECTS: BARBARA BALL AND MAYNARD BALL

Each hand-painted, hand-quilted shade hangs on three rods; the top and middle rods rest in brackets. Lowering the top rods to the middle brackets permits a partial view while preserving privacy.

Silk stagecoach shades roll toward the front, showing off the contrasting lining; pale variegated wire ribbons hold the fabric in place.

DESIGN: FEHRMAN INTERIOR DESIGN INC. WINDOW TREATMENT: OPULENCE LTD.

SPOTLIGHT ON SHUTTERS

Plantation shutters stained to match oak paneling and a coffered ceiling enhance the warmth and character of a distinctive library. Inside mounts preserve the decorative moldings. Horizontal rails on the paired shutters conceal an aluminum crosspiece on the window and allow separate operation of the upper and lower louvers.

DESIGN: JAMES CLAMP, ASID

Handsome painted shutters covering windows and doors, even transoms, bring unity and classic elegance to an airy sun room. The shutters are practical, too: they insulate, control sunlight, and ensure privacy.

DESIGN: THE SHUTTERY OF NANIK

Inside-mount shutters with vertical louvers display unusual practicality: on the large window, two panels fold one way, the remaining panel the other; horizontal rails divide each panel into independently operated sections for flexible light control and privacy. The abbreviated version on the small window unifies two different window styles.

Hardworking Blinds

DESIGN: RUTH SOFORENKO ASSOCIATES. ARCHITECT: HEIDI HANSON, AIA

Vertical blinds with fabric strips inserted into grooved vanes offer the best of both worlds—the look and feel of fabric and the energy efficiency of the vanes' vinyl backing.

DESIGN: LOUVERDRAPE

Light streams through bleached wood blinds covering sliding French doors and fixed sidelights. To unify the treatment visually, the four sets of blinds are hung from a single custom headrail. Above, a demi-round window and a grouping of awning windows permit a high-level view and admit warmth and light deep into the room.

Wooden blinds with twill-tape accent add definition to breakfast-room windows and make great companions to the fabric valance and cheerful wallcovering.

Like undulating patterns of shifting sand, sculpted vertical blinds introduce drama and sophistication. When tilted, the random-shaped vinyl vanes produce an intriguing play of light and shadow.

DESIGN: LOUVERDRAPE

LIGHT DIFFUSERS

Striking shoji screen neatly fits a difficult-to-cover round window, allowing soft light to enter while ensuring privacy. Japanese metal-work decorates the cedar grille; an insert made of fiberglass, rather than traditional rice paper, is durable and easy to maintain.

ARCHITECT: EDGAR R. DETHLEFSEN. WINDOW TREATMENT: HANA SHOJI & INTERIORS

Geometric wood cutouts in translucent decorative screens seem to dance in space; polyester stretched over the frames and then lacquered diffuses light. When opened, the screens stack back completely off the glazing.

A study in texture and tone, a tortoiseshell bamboo shade with self-valance imparts an air of Oriental elegance. Black borders and tassels lend depth and definition to the treatment.

DESIGN: JULIE ATWOOD DESIGN & RESTORATION. WINDOW TREATMENT: LUN-ON COMPANY

WINNING COMBINATIONS

When this sitting area went slightly exotic with new upholstery and bamboo furniture, the traditional draperies—which the owners wanted to keep—seemed slightly out of sync. But installation of a woven bamboo shade tied all together, plus it screened out the house next door without completely shutting out natural light.

DESIGNER: BARBARA ENTERLINE

Scalloped draperies hang in soft folds from a painted rod. Tiny hand-sewn pleats attach to rings that slide on a concealed track in the rod. A cellular pleated shade controls early morning sun and summer heat.

Hardworking miniblinds provide privacy and light control without detracting from the classic swag and cascade treatment softly framing the window. Bows and edging repeat the color of the wall.

DESIGN: BARBARA MACK, FLEECE TO FIBERS INTERIOR DESIGN

Subdued tones and a mix of textures maintain the mood in a tailored window seat retreat. Contrasting damask linings and folded-over tiebacks with cord edging (see detail above) define chenille curtains that break gently at the floor. A delicate handwoven shade diffuses light.

Traditional narrow-louver café shutters provide privacy and filtered light below, yet allow light and a view above. Pouf valance filled with crumpled tissue paper for fullness soften the look.

DESIGN: PAT BIBBEE

Practical plantation shutters complement a decorative swag made by drawing fabric through swag holders and poufing it at the top and bottom of the arch; staples hold the fabric in place between the poufs.

DESIGN: LINDSTROM CO. WINDOW TREATMENT: J C PENNEY CUSTOM DECORATING

Tinged by pale yellow walls, sheer fabric appears delightfully delicate as a softly scalloped Austrian shade; as gathered crisscross curtains, the same fabric dresses the window in opaque folds of fabric. Shirred moiré tiebacks punctuate the treatment with deep color.

Sensational can also be surprisingly simple. Yards and yards of inexpensive cheesecloth wrap a window continuously from rod to floor. When sprayed with a fine mist, the fabric shrinks just enough to form fine, crinkly pleats. Bunched cheesecloth finishes the top of the window; a painted towel ring holds a singular swag to the side.

DESIGN: PEGGY DEL ROSARIO

SHEER DELIGHT

Natural-finished casement windows in a country kitchen get treated to plain café curtains made of semisheer cotton. Usually free hanging, tied back they let in more light and subtly echo the gentle curves above.

DESIGN: CHARME TATE, ASID

Screens made of lace stretched over wood frames fit snugly in the sections of a graceful country Dutch window. The highly patterned sheer fabric provides privacy at the same time that it admits light.

DESIGN: JULIE ATWOOD DESIGN & RESTORATION. WINDOW TREATMENT: ROGER ARLINGTON FABRICS

TERRIFIC TOP TREATMENTS

INTERIOR DESIGNER: SHARI SUMMERS

Instead of a window treatment, this Florida dining room (above) features an eye-catching, eye-fooling mural that resembles draped fabric tied with ribbon (close-up at top, left).

Sheer white voile trims a sun room with soft folds of fabric. The swag is created from one continuous length of fabric pulled through swag holders and poufed into rosettes.

TERRIFIC TOP
TREATMENTS

Small in scale, divided-light casement windows benefit from a diminutive treatment. A single swag of peach moiré drapes alluringly over tapered cascades trimmed with braid.

DESIGN: JANET BROWN

This peaked valance in a bright harlequin print does more than finish the window. It also hides a not-so-attractive blackout shade, which drops down when the room is used as a home theater.

DESIGNER: GINGER MENZIES KELLY

A burst of French country color and
pattern envelops tall windows
dressed in imaginative valances.
They're made by drawing a panel
through two rings, fastening it with
a black wooden bead, and then
fanning it out (see detail at left).
Side panels and bows attach to
fluted poles.

NOVEL TREATMENTS

Where full light is desired but privacy isn't critical, climbing English ivy stands in for a traditional window treatment.

One flowing length of fabric wraps around each fabric-covered pole, creating rounded swags that keep their shape with the addition of fiberfill.

Making the most of a small amount of fabric, an envelope shade attached to a mounting board reveals a smart contrasting lining. When the panels are unhooked, they hang straight for nighttime privacy.

Evocative of the cozy English country style, a single swag with cascades dresses a double-hung window in rippling folds of fabric. Carefully contained within the window frame, the treatment embellishes the window without overwhelming the space.

While this classic room with dramatic draperies and swag valance was inspired by French Regency interiors, the bright red-and-gold check fabric injects a punch of color that is very contemporary.

DESIGN: CHARLES FAUDREE

DESIGN: CLIFFORD MCALPIN

M AKING HISTORY

ARCHITECT: BARRY MOORE

Warm reds and dark blues, rustic planked walls, and simple tab curtains characterize Early American design. Stripes in the curtain fabric become leading-edge accents, tabs, and tiebacks.

Festooned in formal fabrics and elegant trims, tall windows in a 19th-century Greek Revival dining room display the window fashions of the American Empire period. Asymmetrical swags and cascades are beautifully balanced by one-way sheers. Medallions, tassels, and tassel fringe are classic details.

WHEN BARE IS BEST

Upbeat and innovative, this note-worthy wood window consists of four sashes in a single frame. Situated on the north side, it lets in light but needs no sun-shielding treatment. The square panes and colorful frame and muntins form a grid that enhances the sense of enclosure in the sitting area while opening the view.

Handsome casement windows and transoms arranged in a gentle bow were meant to be bare. Built at the turn of the century, the house was situated to allow full morning sun in the breakfast room. Fruit motifs on the wallpaper border frieze and tapestry pillows typify the then-popular country Dutch style.

A little paint and artistry turn an existing skylight well into the focal point of this kitchen. Faux-painted hydrangeas draw the eye up and bounce cool color back into the room. Lighting tucked behind the frame dramatically spotlights the well at night.

DESIGN: TERESA QUIGLEY OF SPENDING WIVES DESIGNS
DECORATIVE PAINTING: N. E. LARKIN AND PAINTED ILLUSIONS

Ever changing and always intriguing, leaded glass is both a window and a window treatment. Hand-cast bevels create a stunning play of light and pattern; hand-blown stained glass contributes jewel-like color.

DESIGN: ALAN MASAOKA

Translucent glass blocks bathe a room in diffused light while maintaining privacy. Although the blocks themselves are small, the windows they build make a strong statement.

DESIGN: LESLIE FOSSLER, ASID/IBD

1

2

3

7

6

11

12

9

10

A SHOPPER'S GUIDE

Even if you have a very definite idea of the window treatment you want, finding the perfect fabric, deciding on the right shade, or locating the appropriate hardware for your treatment can be a challenge. Or perhaps you want to start fresh with a new window. How do you shop for one?

On the following pages you'll learn what's available in the marketplace, where to shop, how to compare similar products, and what questions to ask.

You'll also find practical tips on installing and caring for window treatments. For help in locating many of the products, turn to pages 94–95 for a listing of information sources.

Shown here is an assortment of window treatment components, including (1) pleated shade, (2) wood blind, (3) cotton print fabric, (4) cotton blend fabric, (5) brass-leaf finial, (6) fluted, painted wood rod, (7) rod with gunmetal finish and brass-leaf caps, (8) brass medallion, (9) silk fabric, (10) plastic swag holder, (11) damask fabric, (12) tasseled tieback, and (13) crystal finial.

WINDOWS

The range of windows on the market today is staggering, with new products appearing almost daily. Window manufacturers offer literally thousands of standard variations, from arched casements and old-fashioned bays to hinged or sliding French doors, all with a dizzying assortment of framing and glazing options, some designed for energy efficiency. If the window you want isn't standard, many manufacturers will make one to your specifications.

Windows are sold through many sources, including manufacturers, name-brand dealer networks, window stores, home centers, and building supply yards. Often, the window you order is built at the factory and then shipped to the dealer, where it's prepared for installation before being delivered to you. If you prefer, you can probably find a company that manufactures windows closer to home; there's less risk of damage to the product in transit, and you can work with a local dealer.

How to shop for windows

Take the confusion out of the buying process by deciding first on the style of window you want, then the frame material, and finally the glazing. (Information on those components appears here and on pages 20–27.)

If you're switching to a different style or size, be sure to check local building codes before buying; codes specify ventilation requirements and often insist on enough open window space for access by fire fighters. Also, energy codes govern the percentage of glass-to-floor area.

Operation and maintenance. Look for a solidly constructed window with strong, tight joints and smooth operation. Sashes should open easily and close flush all around, and window locks should shut securely without undue force. Each pane should be fully sealed in the sash, and weather stripping should provide a continuous seal around the window.

If low maintenance is important, consider a frame that needs little or no care. Some manufacturers offer hardware designed to withstand moisture and salt air.

Ask about the balancing system in a double-hung window. Counterweights held by a rope or chain are generally found on old windows.

Among the myriad of window styles available are (1) primed wood casement with simulated divided lights, (2) wood slider with aluminum cladding and snap-on muntins, (3) prefinished wood casement, (4) anodized aluminum slider, (5) vinyl double-hung, (6) wood circle with aluminum cladding, and (7) aluminum octagon.

Newer systems include block-and-tackle (spring with pulleys) and spiral balance tube. A block-and-tackle is easy to fix if anything goes wrong; a spiral balance tube requires more skill to repair. A ladder-lock system, found on inexpensive aluminum windows, works by muscle—you lift the window into a locking groove.

Divided-light windows, which have several individual panes, are good-looking and traditional, but they're costly and inefficient, since they lose energy from the edges of each pane. For a similar look that's more energy efficient and less expensive, you can opt for a grille that snaps into holders on the frame, adheres to the surface of the glass, or fits between double glazing.

For a more authentic appearance, choose simulated divided lights, formed by metal spacers placed between double-glazed panes with wood muntins glued to the glass.

Before choosing a window, consider how easy cleaning it will be. Some double-hung models allow you to remove the sash from the channel. There's even a "tilt-turn" model that rotates to the inside for easy cleaning. Newer casement windows have sliding pivot arms so they can open several inches in from the corner, allowing you to reach the outer pane.

Energy efficiency. Soon all windows will be marketed with labels listing their U value—the rate of heat flow through the window—in accordance with a uniform energy rating system developed by the National Fenestration Rating Council (NFRC). Until these ratings appear, ask for the window's U value (rather than the R value, which relates to a material's resistance to heat transfer). Make sure the value you get is for the whole window and not just the glass.

The lower the U value, the more energy efficient the window. A window with a U value of 0.2 to 0.3 is considered very good, 0.4 to 0.6 average, and 0.7 or more poor. The colder your climate, the more important a

COMPARING WINDOW FRAMES

Wood

Advantages. Wood is traditional, natural, durable, and insulating. Windows can be ordered bare, primed, or prefinished.

Disadvantages. Because wood swells with moisture, wood frames can stick. Wood windows need regular refinishing and can rot if not properly maintained. Paint buildup can make windows hard to open and close, and can lead to air infiltration.

Cost. Initial expenditure depends on quality and whether the wood is finished. Upkeep adds to the cost.

Clad wood

Advantages. Wrapping wood with a thin layer of vinyl or aluminum eliminates exterior maintenance problems while retaining good insulation.

Disadvantages. The inside surface must be refinished periodically. The outside color is permanent and the color choice limited, typically white and a few shades of brown and gray. If you want another color, you may have to buy paintable cladding. Rotting is possible under the cladding.

Cost. Clad wood costs about 20 percent more than bare wood and about the same as prefinished wood.

Aluminum

Advantages. This strong, light material is more likely to keep its shape than wood or vinyl. Anodized or color-bonded aluminum is virtually maintenance-free.

Disadvantages. Aluminum is subject to nicks and scratches. Without a thermal break (a layer of nonconducting material), the frame will transmit heat. Even thermally broken aluminum frames aren't as energy efficient as other types of frames. For this reason, aluminum is used mainly in mild climates.

Cost. Aluminum windows range from about half as much as premium wood windows to about the same price.

Vinyl

Advantages. Vinyl without steel reinforcing is as energy efficient as wood, and new insulated vinyl can be even more efficient. Since vinyl has a permanent integral color, scratches can't lead to corrosion. Many improvements have made quality vinyl frames more suitable for all climates.

Disadvantages. Vinyl frames are usually available only in white, since dark colors absorb too much heat.

Cost. Vinyl windows can cost as much as premium wood windows, but they're not as inexpensive as low-end aluminum windows.

Steel

Advantages. Steel has a modern, clean look with narrow framing lines, allowing maximum visibility. Extremely durable, today's steel windows have maintenance-free factory finishes.

Disadvantages. High cost is the biggest drawback. Although less conductive than aluminum, steel isn't as energy efficient as other framing materials. Double-hungs and sliders aren't available.

Cost. The most expensive material, steel becomes more competitive when used in curved, odd-shaped, or very large windows.

Fiberglass

Advantages. More insulating than wood, fiberglass is strong and durable. Windows come with a white or brown polyurethane coating that can be painted.

Disadvantages. Fiberglass windows are so new that long-term performance is unknown. (The windows debuted in the Northeast in 1990 and will gradually become available nationwide.)

Cost. Prices are comparable to those for premium wood windows.

low U value; in a warm climate, an average U value is fine.

Cost. Prices vary depending on the window type, framing material, glazing, and options. Here are some rules of thumb that apply to good-quality wood, clad wood, aluminum (with thermal break), and vinyl windows.

Standard-size double-hung and sliding windows cost roughly $8 to $14 per square foot with single glazing and $11 to $17 per square foot for insulated glass. Standard-size casements and other hinged types cost roughly $16 to $22 per square foot with single glaz-ing and $19 to $28 for insulated glass. Low-e glass (see page 76) is standard with some companies and costs up to 20 percent more with other compa-nies. You'll pay more for true divided-light windows. Custom sizes cost up to twice as much as standard-size windows of the same size.

Installation charges vary from area to area. It costs more to install odd-shaped windows, since additional framing is required.

Ordering & taking delivery

You need to provide the supplier with the height and width of the window openings and the thickness of the wall. Most firms will send a representative to your house to take measurements and discuss options, but sometimes only after you visit their showroom.

If the window style you want isn't available off the shelf, ask about deliv-ery time. Some manufacturers don't stock all the sizes they offer but build them to order, which can delay a re-modeling job considerably.

Ask for a written warranty and note exactly what's covered by the manufacturer and for how long a pe-riod of time. Be aware that if you install the windows yourself, you may in-validate the guarantee. Make sure you check new windows thoroughly be-fore accepting them.

COMPARING WINDOW TYPES

Awning
These windows are hinged at the top and open outward from the bottom. Often, they're placed above or below larger fixed windows for ventilation. The open sash acts like an awning, keeping the rain out. Both sides of some models can be cleaned from indoors.

Bay & bow
Most bays have one or more straight center windows and angled side windows. A bay with side windows perpendicular to the center window is called a box bay. The windows in a bow curve out, forming a narrow projection in the wall. Bays and bows can consist of fixed or operable windows, or a combination of both.

Casement
Hinged on their sides, casements are cranked or pushed open, usually outward, for maximum ventilation. Since casements seal tightly, they allow less air infiltration than double-hungs. Usually, both sides of the glass can be cleaned from indoors.

Double-hung
Along with sliders, double-hungs are usually the least expensive operable win-dows. Although "double-hung" refers to two sashes that slide up and down in a frame, some so-called double-hungs are really single-hung, meaning only the bottom sash moves. Double-hungs are prone to air infiltration since they don't seal well when closed. They provide less ven-tilation and protection from rain than hinged windows. Problems with the sash-raising mechanism can occur. Double-hungs can be difficult to clean unless you get a model with sashes that tilt inward.

Fixed glass
These inoperable windows come in many standard shapes, including square, rec-tangular, triangular, trapezoidal, oval, semicircular, and elliptical. Fixed windows are the least expensive per square foot, since they have no opening mechanism. But because they offer no ventilation, they're often used in combination with windows that open and close.

Hopper
These windows are hinged at the bottom and open inward from the top. They're often used in basements where the window openings are at or slightly below grade.

Sliding
This is basically a double-hung turned on its side. Sliding doors are a type of slider extending to the floor. Since sliders open sideways and not up and down, they don't need the balancing mechanisms used in double-hung windows. Sliders are similar to double-hungs in air infiltration, ventilation, cleanability, and cost.

SPECIALTY WINDOWS

Skylights, greenhouse windows, and glass blocks are classic ways to bring light into a room.

Skylights. Most skylights are made of wood, clad wood, or aluminum. Watertight joints are crucial. To guard against leaks, choose a well-constructed product and a proven installer. A skylight mounted on a roof curb, a built-up frame, is more likely to be watertight. Don't use a skylight on a flat roof. Ideally, a skylight should take up about a twelfth of the room's ceiling area.

Double glazing is standard and many companies offer low-e glass (see page 76). Most quality skylights are fitted with safety glass. In some areas, tempered glass is required on the outside and laminated glass on the inside; if the tempered pane breaks, the laminated one will prevent the glass from falling. Laminated glass also greatly reduces ultraviolet rays.

Acrylic is standard on less expensive models and on curved skylights. Ultraviolet stabilizers have extended the life span of acrylic to about 20 years.

Screens are usually included with operable skylights, and some companies offer miniblinds or shades.

You can pay as little as $100 for a fixed skylight, about $500 for a pivoting model that you crank open with a pole, or several thousand dollars for a motorized unit that automatically closes when a moisture sensor detects rain. Professional installation will cost at least several hundred dollars more.

Light enhancers include a skylight (top left), a greenhouse window (top right), and glass blocks (bottom).

Greenhouse windows. Projecting out from the house like a bay window but with a sloping glass roof, a greenhouse window can be installed in an existing window opening.

Some models, sold as miniature greenhouses, come with plant racks or shelves. Other models, especially large versions, are sold as variations of bay windows. If you want ventilation, look for a unit with operable side windows. Some companies offer low-e glass.

Prices range from about $500 to more than $1,500 for a greenhouse window approximately 4 by 5 feet. Many other sizes are available, including small over-the-sink models.

Glass blocks. Used where ventilation isn't needed, glass blocks let in diffused light while providing privacy, security, and insulation.

Blocks come in two thicknesses, $3\frac{1}{8}$ inches for interior walls and $3\frac{7}{8}$ inches for exterior walls, and in a wide range of sizes, most commonly 6 by 6, 8 by 8, 12 by 12, and 4 by 8 inches.

Glass blocks are available in such patterns as bubbles, ripples, and swirls. Most block is clear, though Italian block also comes in blue, rose, and green tones, and German block in gold tone.

Glass blocks are usually sold individually and are mortared together on the job. Prefabricated panels are available, but they're very heavy. Installation is best left to a professional.

Expect to pay $12 to $20 per square foot for quality glass blocks. Installed, they'll cost $35 and up per square foot.

ARCHITECT: WILLIAM ZIMMERMAN

DESIGN: KITCHENS BY STEWART

GLASS, FILMS & SCREENS

Here's valuable information you'll need when shopping for glass, films, and screens.

Glass

Many of the greatest strides in window technology are taking place in glazing. Among the new products are double-paned glass that turns at a 90° angle and liquid crystal–laminated glass that changes from opaque to clear when an electrical current runs through it.

Manufacturers have pushed hard to improve energy efficiency. A major breakthrough is a glass system with an R-8 value (R value is resistance to heat flow), which insulates twice as well as the most efficient glass previously available.

Cross section of insulating glass shows two panes separated by a hollow aluminum tube in the frame. Air trapped between the panes acts as an insulator. Often, the tube contains moisture-absorbing beads that prevent the window from fogging up.

But don't buy a window based just on the glazing's R value, since the glass often outperforms the window frame. When shopping for windows, the important figure is the U value (see page 73).

What you should expect from window glass depends largely on where you live. In a cold climate, you want glazing that lets in plenty of solar energy, yet allows little heat to escape. In a warm climate, controlling heat gain is key. In any climate, the glass should reduce condensation, cut fabric-fading ultraviolet light, and be as clear as possible.

Before choosing glass, contact your local building department to find out what type of glazing the energy code in your area recommends.

Types of glass. Here are the main kinds of window glass used in homes.

Flat glass is ordinary window glass (⅛ inch thick is standard for homes). This glass can be strengthened, coated, and tinted.

Insulating glass is made of two or more panes of glass sealed together, with a space between the panes to trap air. Whether having double or triple glazing in your windows is worthwhile depends on the climate and heating costs in your area.

Sometimes, a break in the seal can develop. The best warranties cover a new window and installation if the seal fails within 10 years.

Laminated glass, a shatter-resistant safety glass, consists of two panes with a middle layer of polyvinyl butyral (PVB). If the glass breaks, it crumbles into small chunks, which adhere to the laminate. Laminated glass also helps block noise and ultraviolet light.

Tempered glass, also a safety glass, is shatter resistant and heat resistant; it's two to five times stronger than ordinary glass. If tempered glass breaks, it breaks into pieces, not shards.

Glass treatments. Glass manufacturers have devised a number of treatments to control unwanted heat gain or loss.

Tinted glass, usually bronze, gray, or greenish blue, is suitable for warm climates or unprotected southern or western exposures, where it can lower air-conditioning costs by blocking solar heat gain. The ideal tinted glass has a low shading coefficient (heat blocking) and a high daylight transmittance (pleasant light inside and a clear view outside).

Reflective glass, used mainly in commercial buildings, stops more solar heat gain than any other treatment. However, the view from inside is obscured.

Low-e, or low-emissivity, glass usually consists of two sealed panes separated by an air space and a transparent metallic coating. The coating is either suspended in the air space or applied to one of the glass surfaces facing it. For single glazing and unsealed double-paned units, a coating can be fused to the glass during production.

Nearly as clear as untreated glass, low-e glass insulates a window and deflects the sun's ultraviolet rays. But its chief virtue until recently—blocking indoor radiant heat from escaping—has made it practical mainly in northern climates.

Now, spectrally selective coatings, which reduce solar heat gain without darkening the glass, are making low-e a desirable choice in milder climates. This new type of low-e glass is expected to replace tinted and reflective coatings as the preferred way to reduce heat gain.

Some manufacturers combine low-e glass with argon, a colorless, odorless gas pumped in and sealed between double panes to add extra insulation. The gas improves thermal performance by about a third over standard low-e models at little added cost. Low-e glass with argon nearly doubles the insulating ability of dual-pane glass.

Films

If your window glass doesn't provide the insulation or security you want, you can apply a window film to do the job. Check with the supplier to make sure your windows are suitable for window film. Properly installed film has a life expectancy of about 10 years, though it's been known to last 20 years or longer.

You can install film yourself, but doing it without leaving bubbles or trapping particles underneath can be tricky. You're better off letting a professional installer handle large windows (two pieces of film may have to be spliced together) or any that are out of square or high in the wall.

Don't use tinted window film if there's a defect in the glass; the film will cause the glass to heat up and crack along the fault. Using highly reflective film on insulated glass also causes problems. The pane covered with the film heats up more than the other pane and stretches the glass, rupturing the seal.

A good warranty protects against film failure for 5 to 7 years and covers replacement cost. With professional installation, make sure the warranty includes labor costs. (Also find out whether applying film will void any warranty on the window.)

Expect to pay $3 to $4 per square foot installed, with added charges for difficult installations. If you do the work yourself, you'll pay $.75 to $1 per square foot for the film.

Solar control film. This transparent, reflective film is coated with micro-scopic metal particles on one side and an adhesive on the other. By keeping out some of the sun's heat, it can help reduce air-conditioning costs in summer. The film comes in various colors, from slightly to heavily tinted.

In a southern climate, choose a standard solar control film, which can block about 60 percent of the sun's heat. In a more moderate climate, a less heavily metallized film is a better choice; use it where you want to cut glare and fading more than heat.

Low-e film. This type of film, designed to be similar to low-e glass (see facing page), allows solar heat to enter and prevents much of the radiant heat from escaping, reducing heating costs.

Safety film. Up to 4 mils thick, this film strengthens glass and holds it together if it breaks. It's available clear or with a reflective coating.

Screens

Various types of window screens are available to block insects or the sun's rays—or both. Stock screens cost less than $20 each; custom screens range from about $20 to $70 each, plus installation.

Roll-up screens. Used to bar insects, these screens roll up into a canopy or casing at the top of the window frame. When you want to use the screen, you pull it down along tracks and click it into place.

Made of durable bronze wire, roll-ups solve the problem of how to screen casement and awning windows that open outward. They're also ideal for windows where you don't want to see the screen when it's not in operation.

Solar control window films (top) come in various tints. Window screening (bottom) for blocking insects and solar rays is available in assorted colors and mesh sizes. Darker screen colors obscure less of the view.

Roll-ups are custom-made, since tolerances of ¹⁄₁₆ inch are needed for a tight fit.

Stationary screens. Fixed screens in various colors and mesh sizes are available for insect protection and solar control. Most are framed and attach to the window by hooks, clips, tabs, or tracks. Some are tension mounted.

Insect screens are generally made of aluminum, fiberglass, or bronze wire. A type of insect screen for casements mounts on the inside and has a little door in the screening through which you open and close the window.

Solar screens made of woven fiberglass or vinyl-coated polyester block up to 70 percent of the sun's heat and glare. A screen made up of tiny louvers stamped from a sheet of aluminum blocks even more sun.

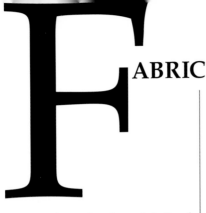

FABRIC

To anyone browsing through bolts of fabric or flipping through stacks of decorator swatches, it's plain that fabrics come in an astonishing range of fibers, weights, weaves, textures, patterns, and colors. Some basic facts about fabric and a few shopping tips will help you select with confidence.

Understanding fabric

Fabric is a material made up of a fiber, such as cotton or rayon, or a blend of fibers. (For details on the most common fibers, see the chart on the facing page.) But shopping for fabric isn't as simple as asking to see a cotton or rayon curtain material.

The same fiber can be structured into diverse fabrics, each with its own visual and textural characteristics. For example, cotton fiber can be made into such fabrics as cotton sateen, chintz, muslin, flannel, gingham, damask, or canvas. The fabric you choose will depend on many factors, among them look, feel, weight, and suitability for the window treatment.

Usually, the heavier the fabric, the tighter the weave should be if the treatment is to hang properly. The looser the weave, the more a fabric is affected by heat and moisture. In humid climates, the hemline in loosely woven draperies can rise and drop noticeably.

In some fabric, patterns are actually woven into the material so that the color shows in a reverse pattern on the wrong side. Woven patterns, durable and generally costly, are appropriate for heavy, formal draperies.

On a printed fabric, the dye often seeps through to the wrong side and looks blurry. The affordable printed versions of such expensive woven fabrics as jacquard and damask now look fairly authentic, thanks to advances in printing. Many fabric mills use machinery that can print up to 20 colors, making more intricately hued, richer fabrics possible.

Although some fabrics hold their colors better than others, an absolutely colorfast material doesn't exist. Bright colors fade more than subdued colors and solids more than prints. The dye process also determines resistance to fading. For natural fibers, vat-dyeing is best, and for synthetics solution-dyeing. Surface-dyed or printed fabrics have the least resistance to fading. If the dye process isn't indicated, ask about it.

Sun rot is harder to control than fading. If the window treatment will be exposed to strong sunlight, choose a rot-resistant fiber. Linen, polyester,

Window treatments can be fashioned from a wide range of decorator fabrics. This selection includes lace, sheer rayon, and medium-weight cottons and cotton blends with woven and printed patterns.

acetate, and acrylic have more resistance than other fiber types.

Common fabric types

Here are descriptions of the most common types of fabrics used for window treatments.

Sheers. These soft, see-through fabrics create an airy look. Sometimes, they're used in combination with heavier draperies in a formal setting.

Casements. Made from loosely woven, textured yarns, casement fabrics let in sunlight but offer a bit more privacy than undraped windows.

Prints. Fabricated from tightly woven cotton or cotton-polyester blends, these medium-weight fabrics are suitable for most window treatments.

Satins and jacquards. Used for formal treatments, these are generally tightly woven, heavy, supple materials that hang in straight folds. Satin is a weave with a lustrous face and a dull back; jacquard is a weave with a tone-on-tone design, often a lustrous motif on a dull background.

Decorator versus garment fabrics

You're usually better off with a window treatment made from a decorator fabric rather than a garment fabric. Decorator fabrics generally have a higher thread count—they're more tightly woven—and stand up better over time. They're also treated with finishes to make them resistant to stains, mildew, and wrinkles, and to add more sheen or stability.

Since decorator fabrics aren't preshrunk, they shouldn't be washed. Washing may also remove the special finishes.

Generally, decorator fabrics are grouped separately in fabric stores. Sometimes, decorator fabrics are identified as such on the selvage (finished edge), or they're marked for dry cleaning only. Most are 54 inches wide,

COMPARING FIBERS

NATURAL FIBERS

Cotton

Advantages. Cotton is stable and durable, resists moths and abrasion, is nonstatic, and comes in a wide range of weights, textures, and patterns.

Disadvantages. Cotton will fade and rot in the sun and can mildew. Untreated cotton will wrinkle and shrink during cleaning; it will also burn.

Linen

Advantages. Strong and durable, linen is nonstatic and resists moths, soil, and sun rot.

Disadvantages. Linen will fade in the sun and will wrinkle unless blended with more stable fibers, such as cotton or polyester. It can also stretch or shrink in humid climates unless blended with such nonabsorbent synthetics as acrylic or polyester. It will also burn unless treated.

Silk

Advantages. Silk is long lasting if handled carefully. It resists abrasion and moths.

Disadvantages. Silk will fade and rot in the sun. It can mildew, wrinkle, and pick up static electricity. Silk will burn unless treated.

Wool

Advantages. A durable fiber, wool is most stable if blended with synthetics.

Disadvantages. Wool will fade and rot in the sun. It also reacts to humidity and temperature changes, picks up static electricity, pills, and must be treated to resist moths and mildew. Wool will burn unless treated.

SYNTHETIC FIBERS

Acetate

Advantages. Sunfast when solution-dyed, acetate is stable and resists moths, mildew, and sun rot. It will melt rather than burn.

Disadvantages. Acetate will wrinkle. It's also subject to abrasion and will pick up static electricity.

Acrylic

Advantages. Acrylic, which is stable, durable, and wrinkleproof, also resists moths, mildew, abrasion, and sun rot. Moreover, it has insulating qualities. Acrylic will melt rather than burn.

Disadvantages. Colors may darken slightly in the sun. The fabric picks up static electricity and will pill.

Nylon

Advantages. Stable, durable, and wrinkleproof, nylon has insulating qualities and resists abrasion, mildew, moths, and soil. It will melt rather than burn.

Disadvantages. Nylon fades and eventually rots in the sun. It also picks up static electricity and will pill.

Polyester

Advantages. Polyester is stable, durable, sunfast, and wrinkleproof. It also resists abrasion, flame, mildew, moths, and sun rot.

Disadvantages. Polyester picks up static electricity and will pill.

Rayon

Advantages. Rayon resists moths and has insulating qualities.

Disadvantages. Rayon is not stable unless it's treated. It will rot in the sun, mildew, and wrinkle unless blended with a more stable fiber. It's also subject to abrasion. Rayon will burn unless treated.

whereas most garment fabrics are 45 inches wide. Often, decorator fabrics are wound on cardboard tubes rather than flat cardboard.

Choosing fabric

The fabric must be suitable for the type of window treatment you're planning. If you want balloon shades, for example, you need a tightly woven fabric that will pouf readily when the shade is raised. Consider colorfastness, durability, and care requirements. Information on fiber content and special finishes is usually printed on the selvage or on the label.

When choosing more than one fabric for a single window treatment, look for similar weights and cleaning compatibility.

An interior designer can guide you by preselecting samples. Otherwise, ask a knowledgeable salesperson for help. Take along paint chips, carpeting scraps, and upholstery samples to compare fabric colors, textures, and patterns with those of your walls and furnishings. Also have with you accurate measurements of the window and your plans for the treatment. (To measure the window and estimate how much fabric you'll need, see page 36.)

If you're shown only small fabric swatches, ask to see larger samples. Unroll several yards; then gather one end in your hand. Does it drape well? Does the design hold its own, without getting lost in the folds? Stand back several feet to see how it looks from afar. Ask for samples so you can examine them at home both in daylight and under artificial light.

If you can't imagine what a tiny swatch will look like as a window covering, find out if you can borrow a larger piece. If not, you may want to buy a yard or two.

Once you've decided on a fabric, buy all you need at one time—and, if possible, from one bolt. Slight color differences among bolts may be no-

LININGS: THE INSIDE STORY

A lining on a window treatment acts as a buffer between the decorative face fabric and the sun, the window glass, and any dust or dirt drifting through the open window. A lining also adds body to the window treatment and improves the way it hangs.

Some linings have special properties, such as resistance to water staining or ultraviolet rays. Other linings are insulated for energy conservation. Still others, known as blackout linings, completely block light.

Most lining fabrics for window treatments are made of cotton or a cotton-polyester blend. They're usually sateen, a type of strong, tightly woven fabric. Insulating and blackout linings are laminated with vinyl or layered with foam acrylic. Most lining fabrics are 48 or 54 inches wide.

White, off-white, and ecru are the most common colors, though fade-resistant colored linings are also available, usually by special order. For a uniform appearance from outdoors, use the same color lining for all window treatments.

If the lining will be sewn together with the decorative face fabric, check the care instructions to make sure the lining fabric is compatible with the face fabric. If the lining is detachable, it doesn't need to be compatible. A detachable lining can be removed when you want more light to shine through the window treatment.

Regardless of how the lining fabric is attached, hold the two fabrics together to make sure that they drape well as a pair.

Interlining is a soft, loosely woven fabric used between the lining and the face fabric to provide extra insulation and body. Since it's heavy, an interlined treatment must be securely hung.

ticeable in the finished window treatment. If not enough fabric is available on a bolt, ask to have a larger bolt special-ordered. If you're ordering from a swatch, ask for a cutting of the current dye lot for approval.

Before you accept the fabric, inspect it carefully for flaws or inconsistencies in color or weave.

Comparing costs

Fabrics sold through interior designers usually cost the most. Retail outlets that rely on sample books generally sell at higher prices than retailers who stock fabrics by the bolt. Cotton prints that sell for $25 to $90 a yard at a design showroom may sell for about half as much in a fabric store, though the selection may not be as extensive. Prices at decorating centers and other retail outlets using sample books vary widely.

You can save money by buying "seconds"—fabrics that have minor defects, though sometimes they're simply overruns. Some outlets sell seconds clearly marked as such; others mix seconds with first-quality fabrics and sell them at the same price. If you see flaws on a fabric and it's not marked as a second, ask about it.

When comparing prices for the same pattern, make sure the fabric is the same. Fabric houses often "downprint" a pattern on a less expensive or flimsier fabric. You may see what looks like the same print priced differently at two outlets, but one version may be on a heavy chintz and the other on a lighter weight chintz that won't wear as well.

Also, remember that in order to match motifs, you'll need more of a print fabric than a solid. The larger the repeat, the more likely you are to waste fabric when matching the pattern.

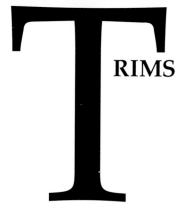

TRIMS

Trims are an easy and clever way to give an ordinary window treatment a custom look or fancy finish. These embellishments range from thick, corded tiebacks and tasseled fringes to ruffled lace trim and velvet ribbons.

Tiebacks and individual tassels are sold by the piece, other trims by the yard. Look for trims in fabric stores and shops specializing in drapery and upholstery supplies, or order them through an interior designer.

High-quality trimmings from a decorator or designer showroom are beautifully constructed, luxurious looking, and expensive—$150 or more for a tieback or tassel and $30 and up per yard for other trims. Trims from a fabric or drapery supply store aren't as well made or lavish, but the cost is much less—you can find tassels for under $10 and trimmings starting at $3 per yard.

Some fabric stores will custom-order fine trims for you if you don't have access to a decorator.

Choose trimmings that are compatible with the weight and care of the fabric or other material used in the window treatment. Bring a sample of the material so you can see how the colors and textures blend. Also, take home a piece of the trim to see how it looks in the room.

Trims are available in natural or synthetic fibers. High-end trims are often made of silk, linen, cotton, or wool, with rayon or viscose sometimes added for sheen.

Here are definitions of some common trims used on window treatments.

■ *Braid* is a flat border, usually 1½ to 3 inches wide, with two finished edges.

■ *Gimp,* a narrow braid, has looped or scalloped edges.

■ *Welt* is fabric-covered cord with a narrow flange that allows the welt to be stitched into a seam. It comes in various diameters, from about ½ inch to 1 inch (jumbo).

■ *Cord* is usually a thick, twisted rope used as a tieback.

■ *A tassel* is a dangling ornament made by binding strands of yarn or cord at one end.

■ *Fringe* is made by attaching hanging or twisted strands of yarn or tassels to a band.

■ *Eyelet* is a flat or ruffled cloth trim with small holes. Eyelet beading has slits through which ribbon can be threaded.

Trimmings that can embellish and individualize window treatments include (1) tasseled fringe, (2) rope fringe, or bullion, (3) tasseled tieback, (4) rosette and tassel, (5) brush fringe, (6) tassel, (7) layered tassel, (8) corded tieback, (9) gimp, (10) cord, (11) welt, (12) braid, (13) ribbon, (14) scalloped lace trim, and (15) eyelet trim.

READY-MADE CURTAINS & DRAPERIES

If you lack the time, desire, or budget for a custom-made window treatment, ready-to-hang curtains or draperies may serve your purposes nicely.

Ready-made panels, along with swags, valances, and other top treatments, are sold in department stores, home furnishing stores, specialty shops, and mail-order outlets. Often, the supplier will also carry the hardware you need for hanging the treatment.

If you shop around enough, you'll find a moderate range of styles, fabrics, colors, and prints. Curtains made from designer sheets and sold with coordinated bed linens are common in home furnishing stores and catalogs.

Emphasis is on easy care, with many treatments made of polyester or cotton-polyester blends. Many ready-mades are lined, and some have weighted hems to help the treatment hang better. Some balloon valances even come with tissue that you can add for extra puffiness.

Remember, too, that the ready-made treatment you purchase can be just the starting point for your window covering. Many ready-to-hang curtains and draperies can be individualized with decorative hardware or distinctive trimmings. (For information on hardware and trims, see the facing page and page 81.)

Proper measurements are important. Instructions for measuring your windows are provided in mail-order catalogs. If you're buying from a local store, supply the width and height of the window opening, and the sales staff will take it from there.

Ready-made curtains and draperies are usually sold by per-pair panel sizes—width is listed first, then length. Some are available in only one size, others in several different widths and lengths. For sufficient fullness, the curtains or draperies should be 2½ times the width of the window.

Depending on the style, a ready-made treatment can be modified for extra-wide windows. Some suppliers sell insert valances to bridge the gap between stationary panels. Some curtain styles lend themselves to doubling up panels on each side. Ask the supplier what will work for you before you buy.

A ready-made treatment can be economical, but only if you deal with a reputable company. Many firms will accept returns if you don't like the way the treatment looks when you hang it, but check on the return policy first.

Ready-made curtains, draperies, and top treatments are available in a variety of styles, fabrics, and patterns to fit most standard-size windows. Here, several ready-to-hang curtains, including two floral prints, a plaid, and a lace, have been playfully piled on a window.

HARDWARE

Window treatment hardware falls into two categories—decorative hardware that is meant to be seen and admired, and strictly functional hardware that does its job under a curtain of secrecy.

Most of the hardware available through mass merchandisers and in fabric and home furnishing stores is manufactured by just a few companies. You'll see the same rods, rings, and finials over and over again. For more unusual items, order through a decorator or look for shops specializing in brass or other metalwork.

Prices range from a few dollars to a few hundred dollars, depending on the item size, materials, and workmanship. You'll find a lot of items on the lower end of the price scale, some on the upper end, and very few in between. It's wise to invest in well-constructed hardware—the window treatment will look, hang, and move better.

If you're making your own window treatment or having it custommade, choose the hardware early in the process. It may make a difference in the fabric's cut length and width.

Rods, swag holders, and other hardware usually come with the screws, bolts, and other components necessary for attaching them. (For installation instructions, see page 85.)

Rods

The two basic kinds of rods are stationary rods for hand-drawn or fixed curtains and traverse rods for mechanically drawn draperies. Within each group, you'll find different styles to serve specific functions or to fit certain window types.

Stationary rods. These include concealed types for fixed panels, rod-pocket curtains, and valances, and decorative types for hand-pulled curtains attached by tabs, ties, or rings. Most adjust to various widths.

Concealed types. Single flat rods, the simplest type, are made with projections ranging from 1¼ to 4 inches so they'll clear other treatments beneath them. Double flat rods are for double treatments, such as crisscross curtains or a curtain plus valance.

Other common concealed types are sash rods, which hold sash or hourglass curtains snugly against French doors and casement windows, and tension rods, which have a spring mechanism to hold the plastic- or rubber-tipped rod within the window frame.

Special types include flat rods hinged to fit corner and bay windows, and custom-bent and flexible rods to follow curves on arched windows.

Among the most popular rods are wide-pocket types, which come in widths up to 4½ inches. Inserting the rod into a heading is a quick, easy way to make a shirred valance. The latest wrinkle is a rounded foam fascia that snaps onto the rod and can be covered with fabric for an instant cornice.

Decorative types. This category includes the familiar name-brand café rods, wood poles, and pole sets, as well as the more innovative, sophisticated metal or wood rods found in decorating shops and designer showrooms.

Decorative rods include (1) round brass rod, (2) square rod with gunmetal finish and brass-leaf finials and brackets, (3) unpainted wood rod, (4) bamboo-motif rod with gunmetal finish and brass finials, (5) fluted traverse rod, (6) brass rod, (7) fluted, painted wood rod, (8) brass café rod, (9) round rod with gunmetal finish and brass-leaf finials, and (10) steel rod with painted verde finish and cast-iron finials.

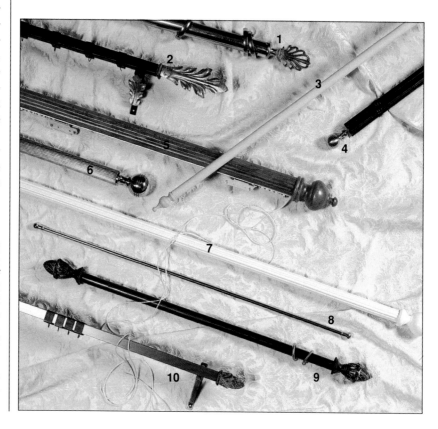

Café rods, usually brass and less than 1 inch in diameter, range from simple round rods to fluted types with ornate finials. Some adjust in length. Rings are extra.

Wood poles, plain or fluted, come in various lengths, diameters, and finishes. The pole and any decorative brackets, inside-mount sockets, rings, finials, or elbow returns are purchased separately.

Although pole sets have a wood or metal finish, they're actually rolled steel. They come in various diameters and are adjustable so they don't have to be cut like real wood poles. All components except rings are usually included.

Traverse rods. These adjustable rods are used for draperies that open and close with a cord. A two-way traverse rod, which moves the panels from the center to the ends and back, is standard. A one-way traverse rod, which moves only one panel in one direction, is commonly used over sliding patio doors or where two windows meet at a corner.

Custom traverse rods for bay or other odd-shaped windows can be special-ordered from drapery suppliers.

Decorative traverse rods work the same way as conventional traverse rods, but they're designed to be seen whether the treatment is open or closed. Draperies are attached to rings that slide on a concealed track. The rod serves as the top treatment.

Combination rods. Multiple rod sets let you put several treatments on one piece of hardware. Double sets include double flat rods, double two-way traverse rods, and traverse–flat rod sets.

A triple rod set, which consists of an outer flat rod and two inner traverse rods, allows you to layer a valance and two draperies, one sheer and the other heavier.

You can create tiers by combining individual rods, though you may need extension brackets to increase the clearance for any treatments underneath.

Accessories

Many shops stock a variety of decorative accessories, such as curtain rings, finials, ornamental brackets, swag holders, medallions, tieback holders, and holdbacks, along with standard window treatment hardware. These items are available in various materials, including solid brass, brass plate, copper, wrought iron, and wood. You'll also find plastic swag holders and medallions that are meant to be covered with fabric.

Strictly functional accessories include hooks, weights for drapery hems, extension plates for mounting brackets beyond the frame without putting holes in the wall, and support brackets for very wide or heavy treatments.

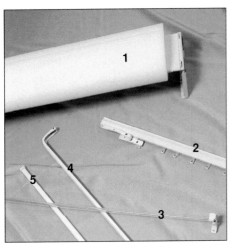

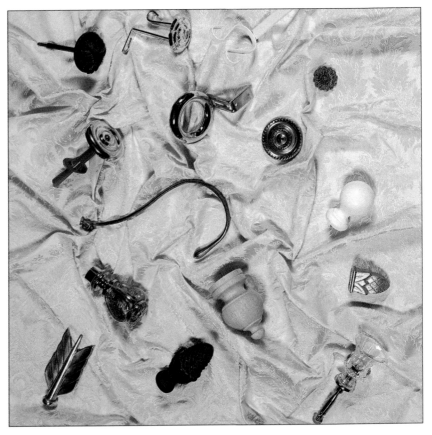

Hardworking rods (above) include (1) wide-pocket rod with foam fascia, (2) traverse rod, (3) flexible rod, (4) single flat rod, and (5) tension rod. An array of decorative accessories for window treatments (at right) includes swag holders, tieback holders, holdbacks, and medallions, as well as metal, crystal, and wood finials in a variety of fanciful shapes.

INSTALLING CURTAIN & DRAPERY RODS

Professional installation for a complicated or heavy treatment is wise, but some setups are so simple that you can easily do the installation yourself. Here are some tips for installing rods. Also consult the manufacturer's instructions for the specific hardware you're using.

Choosing a fastener

For a sturdy installation, it's important to use the right fastener, one that's suited to the surface and strong enough to bear the weight of the hardware and the fabric.

For the most secure attachment, plan to screw into the window casing or into studs. Use wood screws (not the nails that come with some hardware), substituting longer screws for the ones that the manufacturer provides where extra strength is needed. When drilling into the window casing, avoid splitting the wood by drilling at least ¼ inch from the edge of the molding.

If you're drilling into the wall around the window, you have a good chance of hitting wood—the window is framed with doubled studs on either side and a wood header on top.

If you must attach brackets to plaster or wallboard, use large plastic anchors for lightweight treatments and toggle bolts for loads that are a little heavier. For very heavy loads, be sure to screw securely into studs.

To fasten hardware to aluminum, vinyl, steel, or fiberglass window frames, use self-tapping or sheet-metal screws. On a brick or concrete surface, use masonry bolts with expanding plugs.

Installing the rod

In many cases, the length and fullness of the curtains or draperies will determine the location of the rod. Check to be sure that the treatment extends over the area you want covered. For example, place the rod far enough beyond the window to accommodate the stackback if you want the treatment to clear the glass, but not so far that the panels don't close in the middle. If the window is easily seen from the street, position the rod sufficiently above the glass to conceal the heading.

When placing the brackets for the rod, don't just follow the lines of the window frame. If the frame isn't square, the rod will be crooked and the curtains won't hang properly. Instead, position the brackets with the aid of a carpenter's square, making pencil marks on the wall through the bracket screw holes.

Drill holes for the screws or bolts and fasten the brackets securely in place. For a heavy or wide treatment, add support brackets every 4 feet or so to keep the rod from bowing. You can open adjustable rods to the maximum recommended length as long as you use support brackets.

If you're using a curtain rod, simply slip it over or snap it onto the brackets. For a traverse rod, add or remove the slides or rings (you move them through an opening in the end of the rod) so you have a sufficient number to hang the draperies. Then adjust the cord, mount the pulley or cord guide, and center the master slide, following the manufacturer's directions. Cut the cord only after you're confident that you've allowed enough length to pull the panels completely shut.

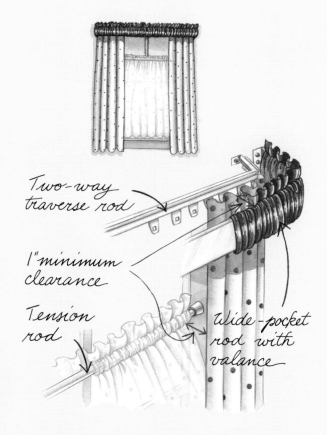

Two-way traverse rod

1" minimum clearance

Tension rod

Wide-pocket rod with valance

Each element in a layered window covering needs at least an inch of clearance between the fabric layer and the rod in front of it. The draperies on the traverse rod will draw smoothly, since there's adequate space between them and the wide-pocket rod in front and the tension rod behind.

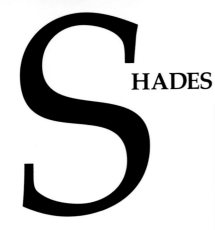

SHADES

Although shades that roll up or draw up in tidy or billowing folds are still very popular, innovative high-tech styles are making inroads in the market. New styles include pleated shades with an insulating honeycomb design and a shade that rolls up but has fabric slats that tilt like Venetian blinds to control light.

Cost depends on the shade design, materials, workmanship, and operating mechanism. Choices run the gamut from no-frills, ready-made vinyl roller shades that sell for less than $10 to handwoven, motorized Roman shades costing thousands of dollars. Most custom shades cost between $60 and $350 for a standard-size double-hung window.

Function is important in choosing a shade. Consider whether the shade is suitable for the window type and size. Decide whether you want filtered sun, a clear view, privacy, or room darkening, and be sure to test the fabric to see if it serves the purpose that you want. For energy control, pick a shade that covers the entire window surface snugly with no gaps.

The maximum width of many shades is 60 inches, though some pleated shades are available up to 12 feet wide, and some cellular shades come in widths up to 14½ feet. If you need a shade that's wider than standard and the supplier suggests overlapping or seaming it, ask to see a sample before you buy.

Make sure that the edges aren't frayed and that the cords or other mechanisms are in good working order. See if the shade remains level when you raise and lower it, and if it stays where you stop it.

Ask about the warranty—3 to 5 years is common for many custom shades. For installation instructions, see page 90.

Pleated shades. Usually all-polyester, pleated shades come in a multitude of colors and fabric styles, including lace, antique satin, and faux marble. Most have 1-inch pleats, though you will also be able to find some with ½- or 2-inch pleats.

Light options range from sheer to opaque. Some shades have two separate fabrics, one translucent and one opaque, with separate pull cords on the same shade so you can switch between the two. Other shades have a thin metallic backing to reflect sunlight.

Attached to a metal headrail, pleated shades are usually pulled by cord into a compact stack at the top of the window. For special situations, consider types that stack at the bottom or unfold from both the top and bottom to meet in the middle.

For side-by-side windows or sliding patio doors, more than one shade can be attached to the headrail and operated independently.

You can get pleated shades for odd-shaped windows or skylights; for

This collection of window shades presents some of the many choices: (1) and (2) roller shades made from solar control screening, (3) bamboo roll-up shade, (4) fabric Roman shade, (5) pleated shade, (6) fabric Roman shade, (7) woven wood shade, (8) fabric roller shade, (9) fabric Roman shade, (10) canvas and bamboo roll-up shade, (11) cloud shade, and (12) balloon shade.

the latter, the shade runs on tracks and is crank operated or motorized so no cords hang from the ceiling.

Cellular pleated shades. These single-, double-, or triple-celled shades, with their honeycomb design, evolved from the plain pleated shade and are used in much the same way. However, they're usually more expensive than pleateds and are available in fewer textures, patterns, and colors. Several pleat sizes, from ⅜ to 2 inches, are available.

The single-celled types come in a range of light options, from sheer to opaque. Like plain pleated shades, some have a dual-light option, switching from translucent to opaque on the same shade. Practically all double- and triple-celled shades are translucent, though opaque versions are now available also.

A major selling point is energy efficiency, with manufacturers claiming high R values (resistance to heat flow). But don't expect the shade to solve your energy problems if your window is drafty and you keep the shade raised or allow light gaps. (For other ideas on how to save energy with window treatments, see pages 30–31.)

Roller shades. Used alone or with window treatments that are sheer or don't close, roller shades provide privacy and block light when pulled down but are unobtrusive when rolled up.

If you want a reverse roll (the shade pulls down from the front of the roller), you must specify it. A reverse roll hides the roller and allows an inside-mount shade to sit flush with the window casing.

The operating mechanism is either a standard spring roller or a bead chain, which stops the shade in any position. A bead chain keeps the shade clean since you touch only the chain and not the fabric. The chain also makes it easy to raise and lower heavy or hard-to-reach shades.

Custom roller shades are usually made from cotton, linen, or other tightly woven fabrics. Solar control screening can also be made into roller shades. Most stock shades are vinyl.

Much of the appeal of a custom roller shade rests in the decorative hem. Some possibilities include a scalloped edge, a braid or lace trim, and a decorative pull or tassel.

Roll-up shades. These shades, also known as cord-and-pulley shades, are flat shades that roll up from the bottom without benefit of a roller. The shade operates by cords that are strung through screw eyes on a headrail or cornice and looped under the front-facing roll.

Made of paper, thin strips of wood, or fabric, this category of shade includes many of the inexpensive (about $25) ready-made shades, such as matchstick shades and rice paper roll-ups.

Another type of roll-up shade is the stagecoach, a custom-made shade that is rolled up manually and secured by ties.

Roman, Austrian, and balloon shades. Roman shades draw up into neat horizontal folds, Austrian shades into scalloped folds, and balloon shades into billows. All have rings on the back through which cords are strung. With some, the pull cord locks the shade at the desired height. With others, you wind the cord around a cleat attached to the wall.

Sturdy, tightly woven fabrics are generally best for Roman and balloon shades. Lightweight, airy fabrics are suitable for Austrian shades. If the fabric is patterned, gather up the fabric to see how it will look when the shade is raised.

Roman shades are also available in other materials, including woven wood (see below), solar control screening, and handwoven natural fibers, reeds, and grasses.

Woven wood shades. These shades consist of strips of wood woven together with yarn. Most are Roman shades, but some are roll-ups. You can usually arrange for a lining on custom shades.

Look for shades with straight-grained, smoothly cut slats. Ask if the wood was kiln dried—it won't be as apt to warp. Polyester or acrylic yarns resist fading.

Woven wood shades require lots of stack-up space. Make sure there's enough room, especially if you want the shade to clear the glass.

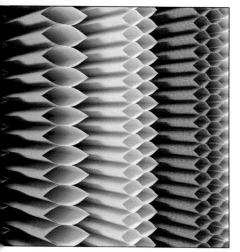

Plain pleated shade, at far left, gave rise to honeycombed single-, double-, and triple-celled energy-efficient models.

Fringe, narrow braid, lacy borders, scalloped hems, and decorative pulls lend interest to custom-made fabric roller shades.

SHUTTERS & SHOJI SCREENS

Both shutters and their close relatives, shoji screens, are elegant, time-honored ways to treat windows.

Shutters. Quality interior wood shutters with movable louvers for light control are expensive, but they're one window treatment that adds to the value of your home. Properly finished, the shutters should last as long as the house.

Traditional shutters have 1¼-inch louvers set in panels approximately 8 to 12 inches wide. Plantation shutters have wider louvers—most commonly 2½, 3½, or 4½ inches—set in panels roughly 15 to 36 inches wide. Wide louvers offer more ventilation and a clearer view than the narrower ones.

Shutters can be custom-fitted for arched and other odd-shaped windows. They're also available for French doors and sliding patio doors. Horizontal louvers are customary, but louvers can also be set vertically.

Shutters can be mounted inside or outside the window frame. Stock-shutter dealers typically recommend an outside mount, since it's easier to install shutters this way and the panels don't have to fit exactly, as they do with an inside mount. Also, some window moldings simply don't allow for an inside-mount shutter installation. However, an inside mount is desirable for a window with an unusual casing.

Quality custom wood shutters are almost always professionally installed; some dealers won't sell the shutters otherwise, since they don't want to be responsible for poor installation. You can install shutters yourself; for help see page 90.

Shutter panels (at left) are available in various sizes, shapes, finishes, and louver widths. French-door frame (below) confines the shutters to the glass area only.

DESIGN: THE SHUTTERY OF NANIK

Most quality custom shutters are made from incense cedar (often referred to as cedar) or alder; both are flexible woods that won't warp or split. Basswood makes a satisfactory shutter, though it's best suited to long, thin elements, such as narrow louvers or blind slats. Stock shutters are usually made from soft, cheap grades of pine.

Custom vinyl shutters, which cost almost as much as quality wood shutters, are also marketed. Their chief selling point is a durable finish unaffected by ultraviolet light. You'll have to decide for yourself whether the look is authentic.

Stock shutters from a lumberyard or home improvement center are usually sold by the panel—about $10 to $20 per panel. Preassembled sets are available for up to twice as much.

Custom shutters, sold through home furnishing and decorating stores, cost considerably more. Top-quality shutters for a 4 by 4 window run between $400 and $500, installed. Planta-

tion shutters usually cost about 10 percent more than traditional types. The price increases with options, such as a custom-matched paint or stain finish.

Don't count on price to help you distinguish premium from poorer-quality custom shutters. Often, the costs are similar. Look for doweled rather than glued joints (two or three dowels per joint signify a solidly constructed shutter). The louvers should be securely fastened to the tilt bar with steel staples and should close tightly. Look for a smooth finish with no paint buildup.

Make sure your window has sufficient clearance for the louvers when they're open. Since louvers tend to become floppy with age, you may want a model with an adjustable tension system.

Warranties range from a year to lifetime, but most long-term ones cover only parts and not labor. A full 5-year guarantee is about as much as you can expect. However, quality shutters can be refinished and are worth repairing.

Shoji screens. These custom-made decorative screens consist of translucent inserts in a wood frame. Although often found in place of windows in traditional Japanese homes, where deep overhangs protect the screens, elsewhere shojis are typically used as a treatment for existing windows.

Rice paper is the traditional insert material, but because it tears easily, it has been largely supplanted by fiberglass synskin, which has a look and texture similar to rice paper. Eventually, the fiberglass deteriorates in sunlight and must be replaced. Other synthetic materials, many of which come from Japan, are also used.

Shoji screens can be made to slide along a wood track or fold over a window like shutters. Several panels can be hinged together and stacked to one side of the window.

The screens are comparable in price to custom wood shutters. You can expect to pay $18 to $34 per square foot, installed.

Four shoji panels consist of rice paper inserts in Port Orford cedar frames. When stacked to the sides, the screens clear the glazing on a pair of double-hung windows.

PUTTING UP SHADES, BLINDS & SHUTTERS

Shades, blinds, and shutters are not difficult to install, provided you measure carefully and use the right fasteners. The information below will make do-it-yourself installation accurate and easy. For installation directions specific to your application, refer to the manufacturer's instructions.

Before taking out your screwdriver, make sure the window treatment fits in the position you planned for it. Hold it in place, positioning the headrail or mounting board at the correct height: the treatment shouldn't interfere with any window hardware, such as cranks and handles, and shouldn't impede the smooth operation of the window. If it does, you may be able to adjust its position just enough to avoid the problem.

Window treatments, especially heavy ones, must be securely fastened to the window or wall. For help in choosing the right fastener, see page 85.

If you have different brackets for inside and outside mounts, be sure to use the appropriate ones. Since your window frames may not be perfectly square, use a carpenter's level to position the brackets or hinges; then mark the screw holes with a pencil. Drill holes to accommodate the screws or bolts, and securely fasten the brackets or hinges to the mounting surface.

Shades & blinds

Most shades and blinds come with a pair of brackets, and very wide or heavy treatments with support brackets. Once you've attached the brackets to the mounting surface, you usually slide the shade or blind onto the bracket or snap it into place.

If you need extra clearance, use shims or projection brackets to hold the treatment away from the wall or window casing. Some blinds and shades, especially those mounted on a door or hinged window, also come with hold-down brackets to keep the bottom stationary. Don't use brackets to keep pleated or cellular shades from being windblown, since doing so can twist and damage the shade.

Shutters

Installing inside-mount shutters is tricky if the window isn't perfectly square (to check your windows, use a carpenter's square, as shown at right). To make the panels fit, you'll have to trim or shim them. You'll also need to nail stops (strips of wood) to the inside top and bottom of the window frame to keep the panels from swinging into the

glazing and breaking the hinges. If your window is severely out of square, use an outside mount.

With an outside mount, you can either screw the shutter hinges directly to the window casing or attach them to a frame that you build and screw into the casing.

Another way to install shutters is to use a hanging strip; screw it to the window jamb for an inside mount, as shown below, or to the window casing for an outside mount. Some companies that market shutter panels sell hanging kits, which contain hanging strips, hinges, and screws. Or you can buy preassembled stock shutters with the panels and hanging strips hinged together.

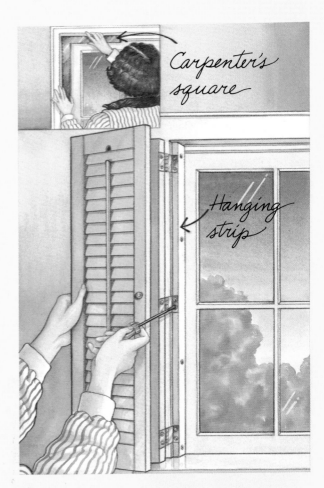

Check window jambs with a carpenter's square (see inset). If fairly square, you can use an inside mount, attaching the shutters to a hanging strip screwed to the jamb, as shown. If not square, use an outside mount, securing the strip to the window casing.

B LINDS

With most window coverings, it's all or nothing. When the treatment is drawn over a window, you can't adjust the amount of light that enters. But with blinds, you can tilt the slats at various angles to let in the desired amount of light, or you can dim the room completely. The slats stack out of the way when you want the window uncovered.

Once dominated by Venetian blinds, the world of blinds now embraces many styles of vertical and horizontal blinds in various materials and slat widths.

Any window blind is only as good as its operating mechanism, so give display models a workout before buying. Make sure the blind opens and closes smoothly and quietly. The slats should tilt uniformly. As you draw the blind, it should remain level and hold in place where you stop it. The hardware should be sturdy and well constructed with no rough edges.

Stock blinds are fine if you can locate ones that fit your window opening perfectly. Otherwise, opt for made-to-measure blinds, especially if you want them for an inside mount. Even at custom prices, most blinds are very economical.

Prices vary widely depending on where you shop and what options you want. Generally, wood blinds are the most expensive, vinyl miniblinds the least costly. Vertical blinds with high-quality fabric inserts can cost as much

Painted wood blinds have 2-inch basswood slats that are kiln dried to minimize warping. The optional blue cotton tapes coordinate with the room's decor.

as wood blinds, but plain PVC verticals can be priced as low as miniblinds.

Some companies offer limited warranties; others promise to repair or replace defective blinds for as long as you own them. Warranties don't usually cover normal wear and tear, however. With horizontal blinds, getting a new blind is often less expensive than trying to replace a broken slat.

Horizontal blinds

The main categories are metal or vinyl miniblinds, Venetian blinds, and wood blinds. Less common are blinds with fabric slats and those with tinted polycarbonate plastic slats.

Miniblinds. The most prevalent type of horizontal blind, miniblinds have 1-inch metal (aluminum with a baked enamel finish) or vinyl slats. You'll also find some blinds with 1⅜-inch slats. Less popular are the micro-miniblinds: their ½-inch slats look too small for many windows, and they require a fair amount of stacking room.

Metal miniblinds account for the vast majority of miniblinds sold. They

DESIGN: NANIK

come in an eye-popping array of solid colors, as well as stripes, textured looks, and simulated wood grain and fabric finishes.

Vinyl minis are considerably less expensive than their metal counterparts, but they are flimsier, come in fewer colors, and don't close as tightly. In a hot spot, the sun can warp a vinyl blind. On the plus side, vinyl blinds work well in bathrooms and kitchens, since moisture can't rust them. Their low price also makes them ideal for children's rooms, where they may be mishandled.

You can get metal miniblinds as narrow as 6 inches and as wide as 12 feet; for best performance, a metal blind shouldn't exceed 100 square feet. Vinyl miniblinds are usually available from 18 inches to 6 feet wide; the blind will sag if used any wider.

Horizontal blinds (at left) include (1) 2-inch wood blind, (2) 2-inch polycarbonate plastic blind, (3) 1-inch fabric blind, (4) 1-inch vinyl miniblind, (5) 2-inch aluminum Venetian blind, and (6) ½-inch aluminum micro-miniblind. Among the vanes available for vertical blinds (below) are (1) free-hanging fabric, (2) fabric in a grooved backing, (3) perforated PVC, (4) flat PVC, (5) curved and fluted PVC, and (6) sculpted PVC.

Most metal miniblinds are sold in two slat thicknesses: 6 and 8 gauge. The 8-gauge slats feel more substantial (though they can flutter in a breeze), and there are usually more slats per foot, allowing the blind to close more tightly. In addition, the heavier slats withstand rough cleaning better than the lighter ones. You can expect to pay about 20 percent more for the heavier gauge.

Miniblinds can be custom-made for arched and other odd-shaped windows, and they're also available for skylights.

Venetian blinds. Usually made of 2-inch metal slats supported by inch-wide cloth tapes, Venetian blinds are available in fewer colors than miniblinds. The traditional 10-gauge slats have largely been supplanted by 8-gauge slats, which perform reliably.

Wood blinds. Heavy and substantial, wood blinds come with stained or painted slats in widths ranging from 1 inch to about 2½ inches. The wider types are often used as a substitute for shutters. Although twice as expensive as miniblinds, they're about half the price of shutters. You can order them with contrasting cloth tapes for a decorative effect.

The wider the slat, the fewer slats there are and the less stacking room required. Wood blinds wider than about 6 feet are very heavy to raise, so limit their use to smaller windows.

Manufacturers warn you to expect variation in wood grain and color. Look for quality, kiln-dried wood; it will resist warping.

Vertical blinds

Vertical blinds, which stack compactly to the side, are considered practical for sliding patio doors and large picture windows. They require less care than horizontal blinds since gravity keeps dust from collecting.

The vertical slats, called vanes, are usually 3½ inches wide, though wider and narrower versions are available.

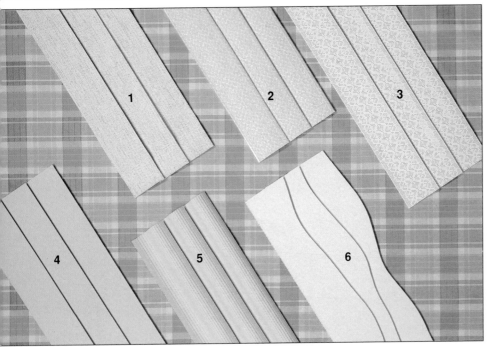

The most common vane materials are PVC and fabric; wood, aluminum with a baked enamel finish, and polycarbonate plastic are also used.

The two types of fabric vanes are free-hanging fabric panels with weighted hems and fabric strips inserted into a grooved backing. You can supply your own fabric or wallpaper for the grooved vanes.

In addition to plain PVC vanes, you'll find dressed-up versions, including vanes with perforations in various designs and vanes sculpted into waves and other patterns.

Look for PVC and grooved vanes with nonyellowing edges; they'll remain attractive longer.

When vertical blinds first came on the market, they had chains at the bottom to hold the vanes in place. Updated styles have made the chains unnecessary, so avoid them—they're a nuisance, attracting small children and pets and breaking easily.

Test a vertical blind for sturdiness. The blind shouldn't jam if you accidentally pull the traverse cord while the vanes are closed. Tug on the vanes to make sure the attachment to the headrail is secure. Still, the hangers holding the vanes can break, so find out if they're replaceable.

CARE & CLEANING TIPS

Your window treatments will look better and last longer if they're cared for properly. Many manufacturers provide cleaning and maintenance instructions for their products. For additional information, refer to the tips below.

■ Some draperies and Roman or Austrian shades need "dressing" to train them into pleats or folds. To do this, smooth the fabric into place by hand as you draw the draperies or raise the shades. Eventually, the treatment will form precise pleats or folds on its own. For a quick way to train draperies, see the drawing at right.

■ Most drapery and curtain materials need to be dry-cleaned, but do so infrequently since harsh chemicals can harm some fabrics.

To lengthen the time between dry cleanings, vacuum often. Once or twice a year, tumble the panels in the clothes dryer. To avoid removing all the drapery hooks, secure the hem over the hooks with safety pins. Add a dry, all-cotton terry cloth towel and, unless the fabric contains polyester, a fabric softener sheet. Set the dryer on "no-heat" or "air fluff" for about 30 minutes. Remove and hang the draperies immediately.

For washable curtains, hand wash them, a panel at a time, in sudsy water comfortably hot to the touch. Drain the water as soon as it turns dirty; then rinse. Wash and rinse again. Hang to dry; touch up with an iron if needed.

■ Keep window shades clean by vacuuming them often. To remove stains from pleated and cellular pleated shades, lightly sponge them with mild detergent and lukewarm water. Check the manufacturer's instructions for the proper way to remove stains from other types of shades.

■ Clean blinds by dusting them with a clean, soft cloth or vacuuming with a soft brush attachment. To clean both surfaces, go over the blinds with the slats tilted up and then down, but not completely closed.

To keep stained wood blinds in good condition, dab wood furniture oil on the cloth when you dust. Metal, vinyl, and PVC blinds can be cleaned with a damp cloth and mild detergent; wipe dry immediately to prevent spotting. Vinyl miniblinds can be immersed in the bathtub, but dunking metal blinds can cause rusting.

To avoid scratching polycarbonate plastic blinds, use a very soft cloth and an extremely diluted, mild detergent or a cleaner recommended for computer screens.

To train draperies, open the panels completely and, with your fingers, smooth the fabric into pleats or folds. Tie in place with soft fabric strips. After a few days, remove the ties.

INFORMATION SOURCES

The manufacturers and distributors listed here are among the many sources of valuable ideas and information about window treatments and windows. They can also direct you to local outlets and distributors for their products. To find additional sources, such as home furnishing stores and fabric shops in your area, consult the Yellow Pages of your telephone directory.

Mail-order suppliers, many of whom advertise in newspapers and decorating magazines, are another option for customers who know exactly what they want. However, if you need help in choosing a window treatment or want to deal with a company that can also install the treatment, you may prefer to shop in person at a local store or to work with a decorator.

BLINDS & SHADES

Appropriate Technology Corp.
PO Box 975
Brattleboro, VT 05301
(802) 257-4500
(Solar and quilted insulating shades)

Beauti-Vue Products
8555 194th Avenue
Bristol, WI 53104
(800) 558-9431

Conrad Handwoven Window & Wall Coverings
575 Tenth Street
San Francisco, CA 94103
(415) 626-3303

Del Mar Window Coverings
PO Box 70
Westminster, CA 92683
(800) 345-3900

Graber Industries
7549 Graber Road
Middleton, WI 53562
(800) 356-9102

Hunter Douglas Window Fashions
2 Park Way and Route 17 South
Upper Saddle River, NJ 07458
(800) 444-8844

Joanna
8701 Red Oak Boulevard
Charlotte, NC 28217
(800) 800-7878

Kirsch Co.
309 North Prospect Street
Sturgis, MI 49091
(800) 528-1407

Levolor Corp.
595 Lawrence Expressway
Sunnyvale, CA 94086
(800) 821-1786

LouverDrape
1100 Colorado Avenue
Santa Monica, CA 90401
(800) 421-6666

Nanik
7200 Stewart Avenue
Wausau, WI 54401
(800) 422-4544
(Horizontal and vertical blinds)

3 Day Blinds
2220 East Cerritos Avenue
Anaheim, CA 92806
(800) 966-3DAY

Verosol USA Inc.
PO Box 517
Pittsburgh, PA 15230
(800) VEROSOL
(Pleated shades)

Warm Products, Inc.
16120 Woodinville Redmond Road #5
Woodinville, WA 98072
(800) 234-WARM
(Quilted insulating shades)

DECORATIVE SCREENS

Blue Horizons
205 Florida Street
San Francisco, CA 94103
(415) 626-1602

Design 1990s
8 Sheppards Way
Kittery Point, ME 03905
(207) 439-8432

Design Shoji
841 Kaynyne, Unit B
Redwood City, CA 94063
(415) 363-0898

Hana Shoji & Interiors
1815 Clement Avenue
Alameda, CA 94501
(510) 523-1851

GLASS

National Glass Association
8200 Greensboro Drive
McLean, VA 22102
(703) 442-4890

GLASS BLOCKS

Glashaus Inc.
Weck Glass Blocks
415 West Golf Road, Suite 13
Arlington Heights, IL 60005
(708) 640-6910

New High Glass
Iperfan Glass Blocks
12713 S.W. 125th Avenue
Miami, FL 33186
(305) 232-0840

Pittsburgh Corning
800 Presque Isle Drive
Pittsburgh, PA 15239
(800) 624-2120

HARDWARE

Graber Industries
See BLINDS & SHADES

Kirsch Co.
See BLINDS & SHADES

Montgomery Designs
200 Kansas, Suite 217
San Francisco, CA 94103
(415) 621-7200

Newell Window Furnishings
916 South Arcade Avenue
Freeport, IL 61032
(815) 233-8371

SHUTTERS

Exterior Rolling Shutters

Environment Seal & Security Co., Inc.
2601 E. Katella Avenue
Anaheim, CA 92806
(714) 635-5775

SHUTTERS

Exterior Rolling Shutters

Environmental Seal & Security Co., Inc.
1640 South Claudina Way
Anaheim, CA 92805
(714) 635-5775

European Rolling Shutters
404 Umbarger Road
San Jose, CA 95111
(408) 629-3740

Insolroll
637 South Pierce Ave.
Louisville, CO 80027
(800) 447-5534

Interior Shutters

Danmer Custom Shutters
9134 Independent
Chatsworth, CA 91311
(800) 445-5333

Joanna
See BLINDS & SHADES

Mastercraft Industries, Inc.
120 West Allen Street
Rice Lake, WI 54868
(715) 234-8111
www.mastercraftindustries.
com

Nanik
See BLINDS & SHADES

Ohline Corp.
1930 West 139th Street
Gardena, CA 90249
(310) 327-4630

SKYLIGHTS

Andersen Windows, Inc
104th Avenue
Bayport, MN 55003
(800) 426-4261
www.andersencorp.com

Marvin Windows
P.O. Box 100
Warroad, MN 56763
(800) 346-5128

Velux-America Inc.
P.O. Box 5001
Greenwood, SC 29648
(800) 88-VELUX

Wenco Windows
335 Commerce Drive
Mt. Vernon, OH 43050
(614) 397-3403

TRIMS

Brimar, Inc.
1500 Old Deerfield Road
Highland Park, IL 60035
(800) 274-1205

Houlès U.S.A.
8584 Melrose Avenue
Los Angeles, CA 90069
(310) 652-6171

WINDOW FILMS

Solar Gard International, Inc.
13770 Automobile Blvd
Clearwater, FL 33762
(800) 282-9031

3M Company/Construction Markets
2100 Wilson Avenue
Saint Paul, MN 55119
(800) 328-1684
www.mmm.com

WINDOWS

American Architectural Manufacturers Association
1827 Walden Office Square,
Suite 104
Schaumburg, IL 60173
(847) 303-5664
www.aamanet.org
(Aluminum windows)

Andersen Windows, Inc.
See SKYLIGHTS

Hurd Millwork Company
575 South Whelen Avenue
Medford, WI 54451
(800) 2BEHURD
www.hurd.com

Marvin Windows
See SKYLIGHTS

Pella Corporation
102 Main Street
Pella, IA 50219
www.pella.com

Wenco Windows
See SKYLIGHTS

Window and Door Manufacturers Association
1400 E. Touhy Avenue
Suite 470
Des Plaines, IL 60018
(800) 223-2301
www.nwwda.org

WINDOW SCREENS

R. Lang Co.
6983 Ave. 305
Goshen, CA 93227
(800) 677-5264
(Roll-up screens)

Screen Manufacturers Association
2850 S. Ocean Blvd #311
Palm Beach FL 33480-5535
(407) 533-0991
(Insect and solar screening)

INDEX

Boldface numbers refer to photographs

Accessories, decorative, 84
Arched windows, 20, **26, 54–55**
Austrian shades, 12, **58,** 87
Austrian valance, 16
Awning windows, 21, **51,** 74

Balloon shades, 12, **45, 66, 86,** 87
Balloon valance, 16
Bamboo roll-up shades, **4, 53, 54–55, 86**
Bay windows, 21, **61,** 74
Bell valances, **6–7, 10,** 16, 24
Bishop's sleeve curtains, 20, **43**
Blinds, 15, **50–51,** 91–93
  care and cleaning, 93
  for energy efficiency, 31
  information sources, 94
  installing, 90
  micro-miniblinds, 15, **92**
  miniblinds, 15, 21, 25, **45, 51, 55,** 91–92
  shopping for, 91–93
  Venetian, 15, 92
  vertical, 15, 22, **26, 50, 51,** 92–93
  wood, 15, 25, **51, 70–71,** 91, 92
Bow valance, 19
Bow windows, 21, **68,** 74
Box-pleated valance, 16

Café curtains, 35, **59**
Café shutters, **56**
Care, of window treatments, 93
Cascades. *See also* Swags
Casement windows, 22, **59, 62, 68, 72,** 74
Cathedral windows, 22
Cellular pleated shades, 13, **16, 55, 61,** 87
Cleaning, of window treatments, 93
Clerestory windows, 26
Climate, 28
Cloud shades, 12, **54–55**
Cloud valances, 16, 27, **33, 40**
Color, 32–33
Corner windows, **12,** 23
Cornices, 17, 25, 31, **33,** 35, **41, 46**
Costs, 36–37, 80. *See also by individual product*
Cuffed curtains, 22, **42**
Curtain (s), 8–9, **40–43**
  bishop's sleeve, 20, **43**
  café, 35, **59**
  care and cleaning, 93
  cuffed, 22, **42**
  custom, 36
  estimating fabric, 36
  hourglass, **44–45**
  one-way, **29**
  puddled, **6–7**
  ready-made, 36, 82, 94
  on rings, **8,** 9, 25, **40–41**
  rod-pocket, **4,** 8–9, 24, **45**
  rods, 83–84, 85
  sash, **8,** 16, **44–45**
  sheer, **16, 18, 40,** 43, **44–45, 58–59,** 67
  stationary, **17,** 21, **26**
  and swag, **41**
  tab, 9, 21, **67**
  tieback, 21, 23, 27, **41, 43, 45, 56, 58, 59,** 67

Custom treatments, 36

Decorating basics, 32–35
Decorating services, 94
Decorative screens, 14, **52–53, 59,** 89, 94–95
Demi-round window, **51**
Design guidelines, questionnaire, 37
Doors
  French, **8,** 25, **44–45, 51,** 88
  sliding glass, 25, **51**
Dormer windows, 23
Double-hung windows, 24, **66, 72,** 74, **89**
Draped swags, 18–19, 24
Draperies, 10–11, 24, 27
  care and cleaning, 93
  custom, 36
  for energy efficiency, 31
  estimating fabric, 36
  fabrics, 10
  heading styles, 10–11
  ready-made, 36, 82
  rods, 83–84, 85
  scalloped, **55**
  training, 93

Energy efficiency, 30–31, 73–74
Envelope shade, **65**

Fabric
  for draperies, 10
  estimating, 36
  information sources, 95
  shopping for, **70–71,** 78–80
Fanlights, **8, 17**
Fan shade, **1**
Fibers, comparing, 79
Films, 77, 95
Fixed glass windows, 24, 74
Frames, window, comparing, 73
French doors, **8,** 25, **44–45, 51,** 88

Gathered valances, **2,** 16, **26, 38–39**
Geometric windows, 26
Glass, 76–77, 95
  blocks, **69,** 75, 95
  leaded, window, **69**
  roof section, **26**
Greenhouse windows, 26, 75

Handwoven shades, 13, **56**
Hardware, 83–84, 85, 95. *See also* Poles; Rods
Heat gain, 30–31
Heat loss, 31
Hopper windows, 26–27, 74
Hourglass curtains, **44–45**

Information sources, 94–95
Interlinings, 11, 80
Ivy, English, **64**

Jabot, **61**

Knot, no-sew, 19

Lambrequins, 17
Leaded glass window, **69**
Light, 28
Linings, **6–7,** 9, 11, 31, **40,** 42, 47, **56,** 65, 80
Low-e film, 77

Matchstick roll-up shades, 13
Micro-miniblinds, 15, **92**
Miniblinds, 15, 21, 25, **45, 51, 55,** 91–92

Natural fibers, 79
Noise control, 29

No-sew knot, 19
Octagon window, **72**
One-piece swag, 19, **60**
One-way curtains, **29**

Passementerie, 11
Pattern, 34–35
Pelmets, 17, 24
Planning primer, 7–37
Plantation shutters, **5, 14,** 22, **29, 34, 48–49, 57,** 88–89
Pleated shades, 13, **16,** 24, **28, 55, 61, 70–71,** 86–87
Poles, **4,** 63, 64
Pouf valances, 16, **56**
Privacy, 29
Puddled curtains, **6–7**

Questionnaire, window treatment, 37
Quilted insulating shades, 31
Quilted shades, **47**

Ready-made treatments, 36, 82, 94
Rings, curtains on, **8,** 9, 25, **40–41**
Rod-pocket curtains, **4,** 8–9, 24, **45**
Rods, 9, **16,** 23, **55, 70–71,** 83–84, 85
Roller shades, 13, 22, **86,** 87
Roll-up screens, 31, 77, **86,** 95
Roll-up shades, **4,** 13, 21, **47, 53, 54–55, 86,** 87
Roman shades, 12, **17,** 25, **26, 27, 29,** 45, 46, 86, 87
Round windows, **52, 72**

Safety film, 77
Sash curtains, **8,** 16, **44–45**
Scalloped draperies, **55**
Scarf valance, 25
Screens
  decorative, 14, **52–53, 59,** 89, 94–95
  insect and solar control, 31, 77, **86,** 95
Shades, 12–13, **46–47,** 86–87
  Austrian, 12, **58,** 87
  balloon, 12, **45, 66, 86,** 87
  bamboo roll-up, **4, 53, 54–55, 86**
  care and cleaning, 93
  cellular pleated, 13, **16, 55, 61,** 87
  cloud, 12, **54–55**
  for energy efficiency, 30, 31
  envelope, **65**
  fan, **1**
  handwoven, 13, **56**
  information sources, 94
  installing, 90
  matchstick roll-up, **13**
  pleated, 13, **16,** 24, **28, 55, 61, 70–71,** 86–87
  quilted, **47**
  quilted insulating, 31
  roller, 13, 22, **86,** 87
  roll-up, **4,** 13, 21, **47, 53, 54–55, 86,** 87
  Roman, 12, **17,** 25, **26, 27, 29,** 45, 46, **86,** 87
  shopping for, 86–87
  stagecoach roll-up, **13,** 21, **47**
  tailed, 21, 35, **46**
  woven wood, 13, **86,** 87
Shaped valances, **10,** 35, **38–39**
Sheer curtains, **16, 18, 40,** 43, **44–45,** 58–59, 67
Sheets, 9
Shoji screens, **14, 52,** 89
Shopper's guide, 71–95
Shutters, 14, 20, **48–49,** 88–89
  café, **56**
  for energy efficiency, 30, 31
  information sources, 95

Shutters *(cont'd)*
  installing, 90
  plantation, **5, 14,** 22, **29, 34, 48–49, 57,** 88–89
  rolling, 30, 31, 95
  shopping for, 88–89
Sidelights, 27, **44–45, 51**
Skylights, 27, **69,** 75, 95
Sliding glass doors, 25, **51**
Sliding glass windows, 25, **72,** 74
Solar control film, 77
Solar screens, 31, 77, 86, 95
Sources, information, 94–95
Stagecoach roll-up shades, **13,** 21 47
Swag (s), 23, **56, 60, 62, 64**
  and cascades, 9, 18–19, 23, 31, **55, 61, 62, 66, 67**
  curtain and, **41**
  draped, 18–19, 24
  holders for, **57, 60, 70–71, 84**
  one-piece, 19, **60**
  valance, **16**
Synthetic fibers, 79

Tab curtains, 9, 21, **67**
Tailed shades, **21,** 35, **46**
Tapered valance, 23
Texture, 34
Tieback curtains, 21, 23, 27, **41, 43, 45, 56, 58, 59,** 67
Tiebacks, **5, 11, 18,** 41, 56, 58, 67, **70–71, 81.** *See also* Tieback curtains
Top treatments, 19, **60–61.** *See also by individual name*
Transoms, **15,** 27, **49,** 68
Trims, **2, 5, 6–7,** 9, 11, 19, **38–39, 40–41,** 43, **54–55, 62, 67,** 81, 95

U value, 30, 73–74

Valances, 16, 27, **46, 61,** 63
  Austrian, 16
  balloon, 16
  bell, **6–7, 10,** 16, 24
  bow, 19
  box-pleated, 16
  cloud, 16, 27, **33, 40**
  gathered, **2,** 16, **26, 38–39**
  integral, **8, 53**
  pouf, 16, **56**
  scarf, 25
  shaped, **10,** 35, **38–39**
  swag, 16
  tapered, 23
Venetian blinds, 15, 92
Vertical blinds, 15, 22, **26, 50, 51,** 92–93
View, 29
Visual effects, 35

Window (s). *See also by individual type*
  bare, **68–69**
  energy efficiency, 73–74
  films, 77, 95
  frames, comparing, 73
  glass, 76–77, 95
  information sources, 95
  leaded glass, **69**
  measuring, 36
  screens, for insect and solar control, 31, 77, **86,** 95
  seats, **2,** 27, **38–39, 56**
  shopping for, 72–74
  treatment questionnaire, 37
  treatments for, 20–27
  types, comparing, 74
Wood blinds, 15, 25, **51, 70–71,** 91, 92
Woven wood shades, 13, **86,** 87